LIVERPOOL EVERYMAN AND PLAYHOUSE
PRESENT THE WORLD PREMIÈRE OF

THE MORRIS

BY HELEN BLAKEMAN

ABOUT THE THEATRES

In 2000, two great regional reps were merged into a single company. At the beginning of 2004, buoyed up by Liverpool's impending status as European Capital of Culture in 2008, they entered a new dynamic era. By returning to producing on a major scale, the Everyman and Playhouse have reclaimed their place on the national stage and generated an energy that has attracted acclaim, awards and audience loyalty.

New writing occupies a special place at the Liverpool theatres, which are rapidly becoming a hub for local playwrights, both new and established. While we have a commitment to produce the best of new writing from around the world it is with particular pleasure that we present a new play from an outstanding Liverpool writer. Helen Blakeman is just such a writer. She follows in the tradition of some of this city's greatest playwrights, such as Alan Bleasdale and Willy Russell. Like them, she writes with humour, heart, an extraordinary and poetic ear for the Liverpool idiom and underlying it all a strong political sensibility. Helen Blakeman is a writer of both maturity and promise; of local and national significance. We are delighted that this new edition of *The Morris* now joins a growing list of publications associated with these theatres:

PORT AUTHORITY BY CONOR MCPHERSON
URBAN LEGEND BY LAURENCE WILSON
THE KINDNESS OF STRANGERS BY TONY GREEN
FLY BY KATIE DOUGLAS
LIVERPOOL'S THIRD CATHEDRAL – THE EVERYMAN'S FIRST 40 YEARS

All available from the Everyman and Playhouse, by mail order (0151 709 4776), or from the National Theatre bookshop.

Liverpool Everyman and Playhouse would like to thank all our current supporters:

FUNDERS

CORPORATE MEMBERS Benson Signs; Bibby Factors Northwest Ltd; Brabners Chaffe Street; C3 Imaging; Chadwick Chartered Accountants; Dawsons Music Ltd; Duncan Sheard Glass; DWF Solicitors; Grant Thornton; Hope Street Hotel; HSBC Bank Plc; John Lewis; Mando Group; Nonconform Design; Nviron Ltd; Oddbins; Synergy Colour Printing; The Famous Bankrupt Shop; The Workbank; Victor Huglin Carpets.

TRUSTS & GRANT-MAKING BODIES BBC Northern Exposure; BBC Radio Merseyside; The Eleanor Rathbone Charitable Trust; Five; The Granada Foundation; Liverpool Culture Company; P H Holt Charitable Trust.
This theatre has the support of the Pearson Playwrights' Scheme sponsored by Pearson plc.
Assisted by the Co-operative Group through Business in the Arts: North West.
Supported by the Eleanor Rathbone Women's Commission Award 2004.

INDIVIDUAL SUPPORTERS Peter and Geraldine Bounds, George C Carver, Councillor Eddie Clein, Mr & Mrs Dan Hugo, A. Thomas Jackson, Ms D. Leach, Frank D Paterson, Les Read, Sheena Streather, Frank D. Thompson, DB Williams and all those who prefer to remain anonymous.

CRITICAL RESPONSE TO RECENT NEW WRITING AT THE EVERYMAN

KEVIN HARVEY AND CECILIA NOBLE IN *YELLOWMAN*

EVE DALLAS, DAVID JENKINS AND SIMON DONALDSON IN *FLY*

LORRAINE BURROUGHS AND ADAM LEVY IN *THE KINDNESS OF STRANGERS*

MARK ARENDS AND NICK MOSS IN *URBAN LEGEND*

Photography by Christian Smith

YELLOWMAN

*"***** Powerfully engaging"*
THE INDEPENDENT

"Cecilia Noble and Kevin Harvey's dazzling performances are compassionate, intelligent and tough... Brighter than that Southern sunshine"
THE TIMES

FLY

"If the quality of Fly is anything to go by, the Everyman's future looks bright."
DAILY POST

*"Katie Douglas's debut play… hooks the emotional heart of a situation and reels it in with dialogue as taut as a straining fishing line. ****"*
THE GUARDIAN

THE KINDNESS OF STRANGERS

*"**** The Everyman could wish for no finer 40th anniversary present than a return to form."*
THE GUARDIAN

URBAN LEGEND

"Laurence Wilson is another name to add to the theatre's long and glorious reputation for nurturing new talent"
LIVERPOOL ECHO

CREDITS

THE CAST (IN ALPHABETICAL ORDER)

Sharon	Leanne Best
Donna	Laura Dos Santos
Jamie Lee	Kay Lyon
Lily	Tina Malone
Margy	Sarah White

THE COMPANY

Writer	Helen Blakeman
Director	Indhu Rubasingham
Designer	Mike Britton
Lighting Designer	Philip Gladwell
Sound Designer	Crispian Covell
Video Projection Designer	Arnim Freiss
Costume Supervisor	Jacquie Davies
Morris Trainer	Pat Hart
Casting Director	Julia Horan
Production Manager	Sam Kent
Company Stage Manager	Jamie Byron
Deputy Stage Manager	Nina Dilley
Assistant Stage Manager	Jo Heffernan
Lighting Operator	Marc Williams
Sound Operator	Sean Pritchard
Stage Crew	Lindsey Bell
	Mary Cummings
Set Construction	Liverpool Everyman and Playhouse Workshop
Cover Photography	Alexandra Wolkowicz

Thanks to: Welsh College of Horticulture, Billy Meall and The Valencia Morris Dancers, Kirkby.

CAST (IN ALPHABETICAL ORDER)

Leanne Best
Sharon

Leanne's theatre credits include: *Solitary Confinement* (King's Head Theatre); *Popcorn* (Liverpool Playhouse); *Julius Caesar, Nicholas Nickleby, Live Like Pigs, Our Country's Good, Platanov* and *The Crucible* (LIPA).

Television include: *Casualty, Heatwave, Wire in the Blood, Memory of Water* and *Casbah – A Documentary*.

Radio includes: *The Importance of Being Earnest*.

Laura Dos Santos
Donna

Laura graduated from LAMDA in July 2004.

Laura's theatre credits include: *The Revenger's Tragedy, The Physicists, Maggie May, Collateral Damage* and *Translations* (LAMDA).

Television credits include: *Fingersmith* and *Innocent Party*.

Kay Lyon
Jamie Lee

Kay's theatre credits include: *How Love is Spelt* (The Bush Theatre).

Television credits include: *North and South, Mr Harvey Lights a Candle* and *Pleasureland* (Winner of RTS Best Newcomer 2004).

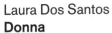

Tina Malone
Lily

Tina's theatre credits include: *Mum's the Word* (national tour) and *Guiding Star* (National Theatre and Liverpool Everyman).

Television credits include: *Fingersmith, Shameless, Between the Lines, Sinbin, Harry Enfield Show, Nice Guy Eddie, Star Hunter, Tough Love, Dinner Ladies, Nature Boy, Something for the Weekend, Brookside, Common as Muck* and *Liver Birds.*

Film includes: *The Long Day Closes, Blonde First, Comfort Zone, Married to Malcolm, Henry VIII* and *Strictly Paranormal.*

Sarah White
Margy

Sarah's theatre credits include: *Mum's the Word* (national tour); *Abigail's Party* (Torch Theatre); *Aladdin* (New Brighton Floral Pavilion); *Stage Door* and *Working Out* (Lilian Baylis Theatre); *Snow White and the Seven Dwarves* (North Wales Theatre and Neptune Theatre) and *Fondant Fancies and Forbidden Fruits* (Old Red Lion).

Television includes: *Doctors, Brookside* and *Overlanders.*

Film includes: *Tom Cat* and *Ice Cream Jesus.*

COMPANY

Helen Blakeman **Writer**

Helen has an MA in Playwriting from Birmingham University and a Degree in Drama from Liverpool John Moores University.

Helen's theatre writing credits include: *Caravan* (Bush Theatre, London and Liverpool Everyman) for which she received the Pearson Award 1997, George Devine Award 1998 and nominated for Playwright of the Year; *Normal* (Bush Theatre) for which she received the Pearson Award for best play 2000.

Television writing credits include: *Pleasureland* for which she was nominated for both a Royal Television Society and a BAFTA Award.

Helen is currently working on a number of film projects for both the BBC and Channel 4. She is also under commission for the Royal Court Theatre, London.

Indhu Rubasingham **Director**

Indhu trained at Hull University.

Indhu's directing credits include: *Anna in the Tropics* (Hampstead Theatre and Scamp productions); *Romeo and Juliet* (Chichester Festival Theatre); *The Misanthrope* and *Secret Rapture* (The Minerva, Chichester); *Clubland*, *Lift Off* and *The Crutch* (Royal Court); *The Ramayana* (National Theatre and Birmingham Rep); *The Waiting Room* (National Theatre); *Time of Fire* and *Kaahini* (Birmingham Rep); *Startstruck* (Tricycle Theatre); *Shakuntala* and *Sugar Dollies* (The Gate Theatre); *A Doll's House* (Young Vic Studio); *Voices on the Wind* (National Theatre Studio); *The No Boys' Cricket Club*, *D'Yer Eat with yer Fingers?!* Part One and Part Two and *Party Girls* (Theatre Royal Stratford East); *A River Sutra* (co-produced by the National at 3 Mill Island Studio); *Yellowman* (Liverpool Everyman and Playhouse and Hampstead Theatre) and Associate Director for *Bombay Dreams* (Apollo Theatre).

Opera credits include: *Another America: Fire by Errollyn Wallen* (Sadlers Wells).

Other work includes: A Granada Artist-in-Residence at UCDavis, California where she directed Ionesco's *Rhinoceros*. She has held Associate Director positions at both Birmingham Rep and The Gate Theatre, London.

Mike Britton **Designer**

Since graduating from Wimbledon School of Art, Mike's design work includes: *Antony and Cleopatra* (national tour); *The Secret Rapture* and *Faith Healer* (Questors Theatre, London); *The Life and Adventures of Nicholas Nickleby* (Milton Keynes), *The House of Blue Leaves* (Central School of Speech and Drama); *Who's Afraid of Virginia Woolf?* (Oxford Playhouse); *The Age of Consent* (Pleasance, Edinburgh Festival and The Bush Theatre); *Madness in Valencia* (RSC, The Other Place); *Dancing at Lughnasa* (Watermill Theatre and Greenwich); *The Triumph of Love, The Gentleman From Olmedo* and *The Venetian Twins* (all at the Watermill Theatre); world première of *Bird Calls* (Sheffield Crucible Studio); *John Bull's Other Island* (Lyric Theatre Belfast); *Troilus and Cressida* (Guildhall) and *Dr Faustus* (Liverpool Everyman and Playhouse).

Mike's future plans include: *The Comedy of Errors* (Sheffield Crucible) and *Twelfth Night* (Theatre Royal Plymouth).

Philip Gladwell **Lighting Designer**

Philip's recent work includes: *A Whistle in the Dark* (Glasgow Citizens); *Aladdin* (Hackney Empire); *HOTBOI* (Glasgow Citizens and Soho Theatre); *Bad Girls* (musical workshop); *Bread and Butter* (Tricycle Theatre); *Awakening* and *Another America: Fire* (Sadlers Wells); *Interior, Winners, The Exception and the Rule* and *The New Tenant* (all as part of the Young Vic's Direct Action); *The Soul of Chi'en Nu Leaves Her Body* and *When The World Was Green* (Young Vic); *Mother Courage and Her Children* (Nottingham Playhouse, Ipswich and Bristol Old Vic); *The Tempest* (National Theatre); London Talent 2003 and 2004 (Big Foot Theatre); *Tape* (Soho Theatre); *Dreams from a Summerhouse* (Watermill); *Way Upstream* (Derby Playhouse); *Dead Funny* (Nottingham Playhouse); *Live from Golgotha* (The Drill Hall); *Passion* (Chelsea Theatre); *Modern Love* (Queen Elizabeth Hall) and *The Soldiers Tale* and *Unite for the Future* (Old Vic Theatre).

Crispian Covell **Sound Designer**

Crispian trained at the Guildhall School of Music and Drama.

Crispian's sound designs include: *Full Circle* (UK tour); *Romeo and Juliet* (Vesturport Theatre Company at the Young Vic); *Neville's Island* (Liverpool Playhouse); *Crossing Jerusalem* (Tricycle Theatre); *My One and Only* (Associate Sound Designer, Piccadilly Theatre). For the Young Vic: *Hobson's Choice, The Daughter in Law, Dr Faustus, Monkey! A Tale from China* (London and UK tour); *Andorra, A Raisin in the Sun, Julius Caesar* (London and Tokyo), *The Nativity* and *Arabian Nights* (Young Vic Theatre's UK, Broadway and international tour).

Other projects include: *The Woman in White* (West End); *Starlight Express* (UK tour); *Aladdin* (Old Vic Pantomime 2004/5); *Tell Me On A Sunday* (UK tour); *Saturday Night Fever* (UK tour); *Jerry Springer the Opera* (National Theatre); *Dance of Death* (Lyric Theatre); *Absolutely* (Perhaps) (The Wyndhams Theatre); *The Vortex* (Donmar Warehouse); *Romeo and Juliet the Musical* (Piccadilly Theatre); *The Tempest* (Sheffield Crucible's transfer to the Old Vic); *Up for Grabs* (West End) and *Cirque Du Soliel's Alegria* (European tour).

Arnim Friess **Video Projection Designer**

Arnim trained as a photographer, AV and lighting designer. His work blends digital media like animation, film-making and computer generated images, integrating them into performances as diverse as Indian dance, experimental opera and children's shows.

Arnim's design credits include: *The Pitchshifter* (Netherlands tour with Insomnia); *Rumblefish, Road* and *Lord of the Flies* (Pilot Theatre); *Life on Mars* (Legolands worldwide); *Amour* (Oval Theatre London and the Dance-Centre Toronto); *Rumpelstiltskin* (Belgrade Theatre); *Paradise* (Birmingham Rep); *Junglebook* and *Merlin and Arthur* (Chester Gateway); *Angels in America* (Sheffield Crucible); *Oliver* (Liverpool Playhouse); *Mozart's Mass in C-minor* (Birmingham Royal Ballet); *My Beautiful Laundrette* (Snap Theatre); *The Wall, King* and *Satyagraha* (Midlands Arts Centre); *Shot Through the Heart* (Pentabus Theatre); *Metropolis* and *The Importance of Being Earnest* (Kaos Theatre); *A Hard Day's Night* (Hull Truck Theatre Company) and the appearance of hundreds of angels inside St Paul's Cathedral for the City of London Festival.

Jacquie Davies **Wardrobe Supervisor**

Jacquie's theatre credits include: *Port Authority* (Liverpool Everyman and Playhouse); *Vurt, Wise Guys, Unsuitable Girls* and *Perfect* (Contact Theatre, Manchester); *Oleanna* (Clwyd Theatr Cymru); *Love on the Dole* (Lowry); *Never the Sinner* (Library Theatre) and *Shockheaded Peter* (West End).

Opera includes work at: Scottish Opera, Buxton Opera Festival, Music Theatre Wales and Opera Holland Park.

Television and film includes: *Queer as Folk II, The Parole Officer, I Love The 1970's* and *1980's, Brookside* and *Hollyoaks.*

Pat Hart **Morris Trainer**

Pat ran her own troupe called St Andrews for 25 years, dancing all over the country and abroad in competitions.

Pat herself danced from the age of eight for Speke Balmoral. They danced under LCA (Lancashire Carnival Association) run by Dick Wilkinson; run now by his daughter Rita Burn.

STAFF

Ruth Adams Marketing Assistant, **Vicky Adlard** House Manager, **Duncan Allen** Finance Director, **Laura Arends** Marketing Officer, **Deborah Aydon** Executive Director, **Stephanie Barry** Deputy House Manager, **Jane Baxter** Box Office Manager, **Rob Beamer** Chief Electrician (Playhouse), **Lindsey Bell** Technician, **Suzanne Bell** Literary Manager, **Gemma Bodinetz** Artistic Director, **Tim Brunsden** General Manager, **Emma Callan*** Cleaning Staff, **Moira Callaghan** Theatre and Community Administrator, **Colin Carey*** Security Officer, **Stephen Carl-Lokko*** Security/Fire Officer, **Joe Cornmell** Finance Assistant, **Mary Cummings** Technician, **Angela Dooley** Cleaning Staff, **Roy Francis** Maintenance Technician, **Rosalind Gordon** Box Office Supervisor, **Mike Gray** Deputy Technical Stage Manager, **Tony Green** Writer in Residence, **Helen Griffiths*** Deputy House Manager, **Stuart Holden*** IT and Communications Manager, **Lee Humphreys** Press and Media Officer, **Jennifer John** Performing Arts Worker, **Shawn John** Performing Arts Worker, **Sarah Kelly*** Stage Door/Receptionist, **Sue Kelly*** Cleaning Staff, **Rachel Kemp*** Stage Door Receptionist, **Steven Kennett*** Assistant Maintenance Technician (Performance), **Sven Key** Fire Officer, **Lynn-Marie Kilgallon*** Internal Courier, **Robert Longthorne** Building Development Director, **Leonie Mallows** Deputy Box Office Manager, **Ged Manson*** Cleaning Staff, **David McClure** Fire Officer, **Peter McKenna*** Cleaning Staff, **Jason McQuaide** Technical Stage Manager (Playhouse), **Louise Merrin** Marketing Manager, **Liz Nolan** Assistant to the Directors, **Lizzie Nunnery*** Literary Assistant, **Sarah Ogle** Marketing Director, **Sue Parry** Theatres Manager, **Sean Pritchard** Chief Technician (Everyman), **Collette Rawlinson*** Stage Door/Receptionist, **Nevean Riley** Box Office Assistant, **Victoria Rope** Programme Coordinator, **Rebecca Ross** Theatre and Community Director, **Jeff Salmon** Technical Director, **Steve Sheridan*** Assistant Maintenance Technician, **Jackie Skinner** Theatre and Community Co-ordinator, **Nicola Sparrowhawk** Deputy Box Office Manager, **Gayle Stevens*** Box Office Assistant, **Louise Sutton** Box Office Assistant, **Jennifer Tallon Cahill** Deputy Chief Electrician, **Marie Thompson*** Cleaning Supervisor, **Hellen Turton*** Security Officer, **Paul Turton** Finance Manager, **Roxanne Vella** Stage Door Receptionist, **Deborah Williams** House Manager, **Marc Williams** Deputy Chief Technician, **Laurence Wilson** Pearson Writer-in-Residence, **Emma Wright** Technical Manager.

*Part-time staff
Thanks to all our Front of House team and casual Box Office staff

Associate Writers:
Maurice Bessman, Helen Blakeman, Stephen Butchard, Katie Douglas, Shaun Duggan, Tony Green, Judith Johnson, Jonathan Larkin, Nick Leather, Jan McVerry, Chloë Moss, Lizzie Nunnery, Mark Roberts, Esther Wilson, Laurence Wilson

Board Members:
Professor Michael Brown (Chair), Councillor Warren Bradley, Mike Carran, Michelle Charters, Vince Killen, Professor E. Rex Makin, Anne Morris, Roger Phillips, Sara Williams.

Company Registration No. 3802476 Registered Charity No. 1081229

Thanks to our Interact team:
Mickey Chandler, Vinnie Cleghorne, Peter Coker, Judith Cummings, Paula Frew, Patrick Graham, Caroline Hanson, Ms Kim Johnson, Chief Martin Okuboh, Edward Terry, Eugene Weaver, Robert Weaver, Ami Yesufu and Malique Jamal Al-shabazz.

Interact is a voluntary group of people working to improve cultural diversity in our theatres as both audience members and employees. If you are interested in becoming a member of the Interact team or need more information please call the Marketing department on: 0151 706 9106 or write to Interact, Liverpool and Merseyside Theatres' Trust, FREEPOST NATN48, Liverpool L1 3ZY.

THE MORRIS

by Helen Blakeman

JOSEF WEINBERGER PLAYS

LONDON

To my mum, Norma,
and all the girls.

CHARACTERS

MARGY

LILY

SHARON

DONNA

JAMIE-LEE

BIG JOAN

ACT ONE

Scene One

A Morris Dancing arena, the previous year . . .

Music plays. A troupe dances, almost dreamlike. At the troupe's centre is MARGY. MARGY *is in her thirties, pretty but sensible. She is the leader of the troupe and this is her moment.*

In voice-over we hear her. She reads a document aloud.

MARGY   'Our Lady All Angels' Morris Dancing Troupe is a youth-based, female-centred, self-supporting, voluntary organisation. Derived from the traditional men's morris, today's 'carnival' or 'fluffy morris' as it is still known in some parts, is made up of a line of twelve girls and a leader. We perform complex dance steps in symmetrically patterned routines using shakers, or pom-poms, rather like those used by American cheerleaders. Our steps are almost like those of the English clog-dancers from years ago or even Irish Ceilidh dancing, as seen in the marvellous Riverdance. The aim of our troupe is to teach our members the art of female Morris Dancing and protect the heritage of this traditional custom, which dates back as far as World War I – when men simply weren't available to dance, the girls took over. We also endeavour to partake in a contemporary keep-fit for health activity as outlined in the recent Outreach for Funding for Charities brochure and aim to be accessible to the entire local community; for all ages, regardless of sex or race or cultural diversity. Our troupe regularly competes in official competitions to a high standard and this year are hoping to achieve our second successive Championship win and become the first troupe to win the double in all our dancing association's history. This is our constitution. Our Lady All Angels' Morris

Dancing Troupe would like to apply for funding
in the category of Youth Development
Opportunities within Sports and Leisure. Our
Lady All Angels' operates an open-door
policy. Please find enclosed a few pictures of
our troupe, including us at our finest hour –
winning last year's Championships. Signed.
Margy MacDonough, Senior Leader.'

(*The troupe end their dance.* MARGY *is
jubilant. Lights fade.*)

Scene Two

*A section of a playing field somewhere near Prestatyn. The
time is the present.*

*A row of chairs set out in spectatorial fashion, each one a
different outdoor variety. A plastic patio chair (another chair
angled behind it). A comfortable, padded chair. A faded, fold-
up chair. A collapsible chair, the kind used for camping or
fishing. Amongst them a few folded chairs lie unopened.*

*Around the chairs, belongings are strewn (plastic bags,
packed lunches, a hairbrush, drinks cans). A couple of cool-
boxes are close-by. At the far end of the chairs, a pile of
holdall bags rest against a large military-looking sack. In
front, a cordon or white-washed line and a pole-mounted
amplifier signify the boundary of a dancing arena.*

*Amid all this mayhem, a large silver trophy lies askew. The
occupants of this area left in a hurry.*

*This is the encampment of a Morris Dancing Troupe. The field
itself is the venue for a Morris Dancing competition.*

MARGY *enters. Same as before, she wears full Morris Dancing
uniform – a short, brightly coloured dress with full-length
sleeves (all trimmed to sparkle). On her feet, surgical-style
shoe protectors cover her white gym-style pumps. Her long
white socks are folded down neatly around her ankles.*

She carries her handbag with her. Behind her she drags a checked vinyl carry-all bag (large and square, seen the world over).

MARGY *struggles on. She pauses, surprised to find herself alone.*

MARGY   Lil . . . Lily?

                    (MARGY *surveys the scene. Setting down her handbag, she claims her chair – the most worn and faded of all. Instantly,* MARGY *sets to work. She retrieves the trophy, tidying as she goes.* MARGY *examines it for signs of damage. Pride of place, she sets it down on a cool-box. An announcement cracks through the tannoy. In the direction of the arena,* MARGY *pauses to listen. The announcer's voice is that of* BIG JOAN, *the competition's chief judge and chairwoman of the Association.*)

BIG JOAN   . . . Can you hear me at the back? Hello? . . . Them nearest the dodgems? (*A shriek of the mic.*) Better? (*She clears her throat.*) Right then girls . . .

                    (*Continuing to listen,* MARGY *goes to her handbag. She takes out her waistcoat – a black garment heavily adorned with medals, front and back, it is the symbol of many dancing victories.* MARGY *dons it, worthy of her rank.*)

BIG JOAN   On behalf of the North West and North Wales International Morris Dance Association, a big warm welcome. That time of year again and as usual the sun's still shining. Well, simply the best is what we are and today girls, this is your chance to prove it!

                    (*A half-hearted cheer is heard.* MARGY *applauds. From the tannoy music plays, possibly 'Simply the Best' by Tina Turner. Suddenly,* MARGY *checks behind her. She hurries. From the rear of the chairs,* Margy *takes up a large banner. She fixes it in place and unfurls it. Framing the camp, the banner reads – 'Our Lady All Angels Morris Dancing Troupe'.* Margy *steps back to check her work. Over the music, the announcement continues.*)

Big Joan   So let's hear it, a big Championship welcome for our wonderful troupes . . .

(*The announcement goes on, with cheers and applause heard after each troupe name.*)

Big Joan   Classique . . . Wigan Pierettes . . . Halton Hi-Lites . . .

(Margy *goes to the arena, she waits expectantly.*)

Big Joan   . . . Speke Jaguar . . . Toxteth Debutantes . . . Milano . . . Our Lady All Angels' . . . Sovereignettes . . .

Margy   (*automatically, she chants*) Our Lay-deez. Winning is our Ee-ease!

(Margy's *applause fades, embarrassed. The announcement continues.*)

Big Joan   From myself and the committee, we wish you all . . . You're all winners to us, girls.

(*Another cheer is heard. The music hiccups to a stop.*)

Big Joan   And on a serious note. Litter. Keep Prestatyn clean. This is a holiday mecca for them what come here . . . so let's hope it stays that way. You have been warned.

(Margy *picks up another crisp packet. She gazes off for signs of life.* Margy *returns to her chair. From her handbag she removes a folder. She takes out a handful of forms and paperwork.* MARGY *sits. She begins to leaf through the papers, checking over every page before resting it aside. After a moment,* LILY *enters.* LILY *is a short and sturdy woman in her forties. She is dressed in leggings and a tracksuit jacket decorated with a spangly troupe rosette. She is tired from walking.)*

MARGY   About time.

LILY   Hiya Marg.

*(*MARGY *puts down the forms, ready to confront her.* LILY *continues to the large, padded chair.)*

MARGY   Lily . . . where have you been?

LILY   Where the frig haven't I been.

*(*LILY *pauses. She kicks off her flip-flops.)*

MARGY   What about the rest of them? Lily . . . where are they?

*(*LILY *doesn't reply. From the cool-box she picks up the forms, she glances them.* LILY *discards the forms to the floor.)*

MARGY   Do you mind? My funding. My application, I was checking that.

*(*LILY *turns, patting up her chair for comfort. For the first time, we see the back of her jacket. It is emblazoned with the word 'TRAINER'.* LILY *adjusts her knickers, sits.)*

LILY   Jesus, you couldn't go forgetting a pair of pumps or nothing on this field could you. Bleedin'ell . . .

*(*LILY *puts up her feet on the cool-box.* MARGY *retrieves the papers from the floor.)*

LILY   What's up? I haven't missed nothing, have I?

MARGY	Not much. When Big Joan started . . . us. Never even got a cheer. Everybody else, oh they had whoops, shouting their heads off. But oh no. Come our turn, what did we have? Margy-no mates, doing her best, as usual, by herself like some . . .
LILY	Knobhead.
MARGY	Yeah . . . No. Defending champions . . . and look at it. I felt ashamed.
LILY	I bet you did.
	(LILY *lights up a cigarette*.)
MARGY	Lily. If we'd have been robbed . . . can you imagine it? Some chance of winning we'd have stood then.
LILY	Margy, there's nothing worth nothing to rob.
MARGY	Not much. Just like a piece of championship silver. Left. Knocking about. Unattended. If that had gone . . . My God, I would like to have heard you explain that one to Big Joan
LILY	Her? I wouldn't explain nothing.
MARGY	What would she think of us then eh? Sold it. She'd think we'd had it pawned.
LILY	She could think what she liked.
MARGY	Lily. You should have been over here.
	(MARGY *returns to her seat. She begins to check through the paperwork once more*.)
LILY	If it wasn't for Siobhan Walsh I would have been.
MARGY	That's right. Blame Siobhan Walsh.
LILY	I'm not. I'm blaming her head.
	(MARGY *pauses*.)

LILY   Absolutely. Crawling.

MARGY   Not again.

LILY   Oh aye. Only this time. Our Jamie-Lee was
                    doing her hair. And you know what our Jamie-
                    Lee's like once she's got a brush in her
                    hands . . .

MARGY   Lethal.

LILY   Honest to God. There. She was. In the
                    hairdressing chair. Siobhan, just sitting there.
                    Like . . . one minute, alright. Our Jamie-Lee's
                    ragging the head off her, all this brand new,
                    you know all this braided and corn-rows what
                    she's learned at the college and the next . . .
                    Well. I've heard our Jamie-Lee scream. But
                    move? . . . By Christ. She went one way. The
                    brush went the other. Lauren's Noodle Snak
                    went straight down her Lacoste, her ma's
                    gonna kill her . . . and the screams. The whole
                    troupe was up. It was a wonder you never
                    heard them from our bus 'cos she must have
                    disturbed a right little cluster, our Jamie. And
                    the eggs, my God. And the mothers, the bogies.
                    Legging. You could see them. Along the plaits,
                    along the parting. Everywhere. Not knowing
                    whether to save the eggs or save themselves.
                    You could, couldn't you Sharon?

                    (*At the other end of the encampment, from
                    beneath her camouflaged position amid bags,
                    SHARON rises from behind the large sack.
                    SHARON is in her twenties and on the smooth
                    side of rough. A morris dancer, she wears the
                    same troupe tracksuit as LILY. The back of
                    SHARON's tracksuit however bears the name of
                    the troupe. SHARON rises a moment, a sparkly,
                    troupe-coloured, novelty stetson sitting askew
                    over her face.*)

SHARON   Her head was visibly moving.

LILY   See.

MARGY   Sharon . . .

                  (SHARON *groans. She rests back.*)

MARGY   Sharon.

                  (*From the nearest cool-box,* LILY *takes out a
                  diluted orange-drink bottle, although the
                  orange drink has been replaced by Coke or
                  some such. She sets it down, replaces the lid.*)

LILY   The thing was, Marg. Nits. It was the perfect
                  frigging excuse.

MARGY   Excuse. For who?

LILY   The whole lot of them. The troupe. It was you
                  what wanted to know. They bloody legged it.
                  That's where they are.

MARGY   Right . . . and you legged after them.

                  (*From her jacket pockets* LILY *begins to
                  remove a neat stack of plastic glasses. She sets
                  them out on a cool-box, party style.*)

LILY   Honest to God. Poor bloody Siobhan. How
                  many times is this with her head now?

SHARON   About the same as how many kids live in their
                  house.

LILY   Hundreds.

MARGY   Underprivileged. Right under my nose. That's
                  another box I can tick.

                  (MARGY *reaches the forms, takes out a pen.*
                  LILY *pours some of her drink into two glasses.*)

LILY   Anyway after all that, it took me another whole
                  half an hour to find the place. But you know
                  Sha, I managed to sniff it out somehow. (*She
                  presents her table.*) The beer tent.

(LILY *offers a drink in* SHARON'S *direction.* SHARON *staggers up best she can to reach it.*)

SHARON   Nice one, Lil.

MARGY   Now, eh.

SHARON   Hair of the dog. D'you get my mixers?

MARGY   I hope that's not fizzy.

LILY   (*passing small bottles of lemonade*) Diet, Sha.

MARGY   You've got to dance yet.

SHARON   Do I owe you?

LILY   I owe you.

(SHARON *pulls out a bottle of cheap white rum.*)

SHARON   D'you want one, Marg?

MARGY   No, I don't.

SHARON   Bacardi. I've got bottles. D'you want a bottle?

MARGY   No. Neither should you.

SHARON   You used to have one. Before.

MARGY   Before a dance? I don't think –

SHARON   Before last year. But one sniff of silverware. Aren't I right, Lil. That's all it took for her.

MARGY   Sharon. The arena . . . Judges.

SHARON   Margy. Sussed.

(SHARON *holds up an empty mineral water bottle. Turning away from the arena, she mixes her drink into it. She looks to* MARGY.)

SHARON   What? . . . Girls have danced with worse things than hangovers you know.

LILY   Whooping cough. A broken ankle. I remember
                my mam saying, there was twins with rickets
                once. They never won nothing like.

SHARON   (*gesturing herself*) Eh. Pregnant and they
                didn't fucking know it.

MARGY   All very well. But today. There just happens to
                be a lot at stake.

SHARON   Margy. I'll be alright.

                (*Testing her mix,* SHARON *takes a drink.*)

MARGY   Honest to God. Why I bother? Sharon. Can't
                you . . . just for once.

SHARON   No.

                (*A pause.* MARGY *sets down her application.*)

MARGY   Well. Some big bloody joke this is isn't.
                Applying for a grant to some big panel, in like
                London. Can you imagine that, eh? If they
                come here to check us out. Turning up here.
                'What was it you was applying for again,
                Sports and Leisure funding?' . . . Leisure, yeah
                we'd pass that one alright. Flying colours. But
                as for the sport.

SHARON   Will you give it a rest.

MARGY   'We are a highly motivated and successful
                morris dancing troupe'. Our constitution. I
                might as well have written a pack of lies.

LILY   Our what?

MARGY   Our troupe constitution. All this. That's what
                I've had to do. Type it out, check it, copy it in
                work.

LILY   A constie what?

MARGY   A document. Everything this whole troupe
               stands for, they want to know. What we're
               about. Everything. Have you ever really
               thought about that. You know, why do we even
               exist?

SHARON   Frig off.

MARGY   I think it's a good point myself. Every week,
               you know. Why do we do it.

LILY   'Cos my mam did it. She ran the troupe, she
               brought me, I done it, our Jamie-Lee.

MARGY   Lily. But what this is all about. Within the
               wider community. Why morris?

SHARON   It's something to do. Isn't it? You come here,
               you see your mates. Just tell them. We have a
               laugh.

MARGY   Have a laugh? Oh, I'm sure they'd really
               appreciate . . .

SHARON   Well. It's the truth isn't it. If it wasn't for this
               dancing, I'd still be sitting on our settee
               watching Most Haunted. You want to put
               something Margy, you put that. Away from the
               kids. Morris gets me out the house.

MARGY   Right.

               (MARGY *returns to the forms*.)

SHARON   What's wrong with that?

LILY   It's not clever enough, that's what wrong with
               it. Not for the University of Morris Dancing
               here. Application? I'll be glad when it's in the
               sodding post, I'm telling you. Last practise
               night. Form. Next practise night. Form. Now
               here. Formed off, d'you know what I mean?

MARGY   Look. Lily. They don't just give money to
               anybody you know. You need to be like,

deserving. The best. So winning today, a grant
. . . it's hand in hand. Just like a business.
Whatever they give out, they need to know
they're gonna get it back.

(LILY *and* SHARON *exchange a reaction.*)

MARGY   Not the money. They want it back in other
             ways.

LILY   Like what?

MARGY   A display every now and then. The odd school
             fete.

SHARON   On a Saturday? After a Friday night.

MARGY   Not every week. The old peoples' home at
             Christmas, the Church club on saints' days.
             That sort of thing.

LILY   All that?

MARGY   It's not much.

LILY   And now you're telling me. All that? For five
             hundred quid?

MARGY   It's a new set of dresses. If we win today, we
             can't wear these a second season. We'd be a
             laughing stock.

LILY   Even so. Displays . . .

             (*A pause.*)

MARGY   I get it. All the success, none of the work.
             Whatever happened to, what was it, some of us
             wanting to get our name on that trophy, eh?

             (*Casually,* SHARON *checks at the trophy.*)

SHARON   Our name already is. You got that engraved,
             didn't you, Lil?

MARGY   No Sharon, I did. But getting our name back on
             it, that's what I meant. Our Ladys'. Our Ladys'.
             Win it twice. And at last . . . This is our chance
             to show were no one-hit wonders like all the
             rest of them. Everything else will just fall into
             place. We won't be just 'some troupe'. We'd
             be 'the' troupe. (*She pauses.*) That is what
             we've been training for, you know. In the
             church hall every Wednesday, every Thursday
             night in your back garden. Or has that just
             happened to slip your mind and all?

             (*On the cool-box,* LILY *moves her drink aside.
             She puts her feet up.*)

LILY   Could it ever?

             (MARGY *replaces her forms into her bag. She
             returns to her place. Slight pause.*)

SHARON   We are 'the' troupe though, aren't we. After
             last year. Last year, I thought we done boss.

MARGY   Last year you didn't drink.

SHARON   Didn't I? Last year, I can't remember.

MARGY   Antibiotics. You tried a few sly swigs on the
             way like.

LILY   But thank God for Donna.

SHARON   Her. Yeah. Donna . . . friggin'ell. What was it,
             some fella in her mother's shop and his liver
             exploded.

LILY   Donna dramatic arse.

             (*From the carry-all bag,* MARGY *removes a
             glittering pile of headdresses. She also takes
             out a large tupperware container. Inside, a set
             of numbered drawstring bags, troupe bags.
             Organising herself on the floor, she begins to
             sort each headdress into its corresponding
             bag. Checking them over as she does so, she*

may try some across her head, maybe give some a stretch.)

MARGY   Sensible Donna. At least then I had someone to back me up. Now . . .

SHARON   Thank God you haven't.

MARGY   Just me against the world it is. All this. Headdresses, troupe bags. Donna, where is she now, eh?

LILY   Had a baby, Margy. That's where she is.

          (MARGY *goes on, continuing her task, she searches for a headdress.*)

MARGY   Exactly. And, soon gone and forgot we are. Had a baby, they all soon change. Number five . . . where is it . . . ? Mind you, at least Donna put the work in. That's one thing I'd say for her . . . Got it. Not the best dancer but . . . reliable, organised.

SHARON   Liked.

MARGY   You see. If Donna was here, things might be different.

          (*Slight pause.* LILY *fills up her glass.*)

LILY   Well, I hate to spoil your fun and that, Marg, but the way I see it. Facts have to be faced. Winning the double, we could have done it years ago. Couldn't we. You know . . . if it wasn't for like . . . You.

SHARON   Yeah. We could.

MARGY   And how would you know?

          (MARGY *pulls the present headdress from her head.*)

MARGY   You were a kid, Sharon. You wouldn't even
             remember it. Just some kid in the tinies. 'We
             could'.

             (MARGY *tries the present headdress, across her*
             head. She checks its number, she pauses.)

MARGY   Number eight? Who the bloody'ell's number
             eight . . . ?

             (*From* MARGY'S *reaction, the headdress is*
             obviously Siobhan's. MARGY *places it back*
             into the tupperware box. She closes the lid
             firm.)

LILY   (*laughs*) Eh, yeah . . . and you were another
             one.

SHARON   Another what?

LILY   Old Nitty Nora.

SHARON   No I wasn't.

LILY   Christmas lucky dip. Margy, how many times
             did I try to fiddle it for her to win the nit comb?

SHARON   Fuck off.

MARGY   See. If you don't even know about that.

SHARON   Know about what . . . ?

             (*Pause.*)

LILY   It was a lovely day though, wasn't it, Marg.
             Like today. It was. And we had it all. We'd won
             the year before, me leading. We was favourites.
             But then Margy comes along . . . her first
             Championships as leader. And talk about
             ballsed it up.

MARGY   No, I never.

LILY   She did. Good and very bleeding proper.

SHARON	Go 'way. You did? Did you, Marg?
MARGY	The taped machine chewed up our music.
LILY	That's right. And who never bothered to bang the troupe back into rhythm.
MARGY	I couldn't hear, that's why.
LILY	Here y'are. Here we go.
MARGY	Speke Jags started cheering.
LILY	Speke Jags? What did I say.
MARGY	They were cheering and they were shouting.
LILY	Go on.
MARGY	Lily, how many years ago is this?
LILY	Enough for me to remember, girl.
MARGY	I was a new leader, my nerves went.
LILY	That's right. And so did our chance of all the glory. A leader's supposed to keep her girls in check during a dance, you know.
MARGY	I know that.
LILY	You never that day. I head-hunted you. I shouldn't have bleeding bothered.
MARGY	Come off it. Head-hunted? Suzettes were packing in.
LILY	Just had our Jamie-Lee, I was desperate.
MARGY	I asked to join.
LILY	And I said yeah? I never had no choice. Double winners already. That's what we could have been.

MARGY   Now, eh. If it wasn't for Speke Jags and you
             know it. They saw us go wrong and they
             couldn't help themselves.

SHARON   The cheeky fuckers.

MARGY   Yeah, well. They always have been.

SHARON   I'm telling you. Sounds like they should have
             been well disqualified, love.

MARGY   Speke? With Big Joan one of their old girls . . .
             we didn't stand a chance.

LILY   No. A right holy show it was. Wasn't it.

MARGY   Wasn't it.

             (*They laugh.*)

SHARON   Fuckin'ell. I can't get over it. You Margy,
             making a mistake . . . and who says morris isn't
             educational?

LILY   Eh Marg. 'Ere y'are. That's another one.
             Educational. You can put that down and all.

             (SHARON *stands, she considers.*)

SHARON   Mind you, not that we've got anything to
             worry about today. Speke Jags, this year,
             we've beat their arse every time. (*She takes
             another drink.*) Ooh. Kicking in.

MARGY   Not every time. When you was on holiday.

SHARON   Er, on business.

MARGY   And Wigan. Wigan's beat us.

SHARON   Wigan Pierettes? Chill out Margy. All we need
             to do is concentrate. We'll walk it.

             (SHARON *goes to her holdall. She opens it.
             Inside an array of wares – cigarette boxes,
             packaged clothing. She rummages through.*)

SHARON	Bloody 'ell, my little stockroom's heaving in here.
MARGY	It's not always as easy as that though is it. Sharon. Is it?
LILY	Margy. You heard the girl.

(From the bag, SHARON *pulls out a change of clothes. She moves away, behind the banner.)*

MARGY	No. I haven't even took the draw. What number we're drawn, the effect that can have . . . Sharon. Sharon. I mean it now.
LILY	*(calling out to her)* What have you got today for us then, Sha?
SHARON	Trackies, Bodrum market. Ciggies. The usual.
MARGY	See. This is all we need.

*(*LILY *moves closer.)*

LILY	Good, yeah?
SHARON	Usual. Same price.
LILY	Smashing.
MARGY	I don't believe this.
SHARON	Only I nearly got ripped off this time you know.
LILY	You never.

(From behind the banner, SHARON'S *head pops out.)*

SHARON	Lily, I am not messing. Four million a packet he wanted for the Regal. I said to him. Mehmet, three and a half like last time or you can forget it. These ciggies, round our way lad, they're not just a bit of fun you know. They're a fucking lifeline.

LILY	Go 'way. I bet he saw his other side, didn't he?
SHARON	He well did. Threw me in a box of herbal ones for nothing. You know, like he thinks he's doing me favour. Herbal ciggies. Have you ever tried shifting them . . .

(SHARON *emerges. She has changed. Wearing tight shorts, a top, she looks good.*)

SHARON	Next time, he said he'll come to some arrangement.
LILY	I bet he will.
MARGY	Next time.
LILY	Sharon International. Listen to her.
SHARON	I know, yeah. But the kids love it. So what can you do.

(*On the grass,* SHARON *settles down to sunbathe.*)

MARGY	When is it you're actually like, thinking of going then, Sha?
SHARON	Dunno. You know . . . book it, pack it, fuck off.
MARGY	Well. Next time. Try to make it mid-week, eh? You know, say a Wednesday flight out, back for the weekend. Either that or you could always go out of season.
SHARON	You what?
MARGY	Our Lady's, Sharon. If we win today, if we get like get this grant. God knows, we'll need you.
SHARON	And what d'you think I need? The money.
MARGY	You'd be back for a Sunday comp, that's all I meant.

SHARON	I know what you meant . . . Jesus . . . It's alright for some, isn't it. You and your husband, rattling round in a semi-detached.
MARGY	Sharon . . .
SHARON	You think about it. It's just not that easy, alright. (*Pause.*) I found out this week. The housing told me. The only three-bedroomed coming up, it's on Beirut Corner.
LILY	Jesus . . .
MARGY	On where? Beirut.
LILY	Sharon, love. No wonder you hit the bottle.
SHARON	Beirut Corner, Marg. The only block left what's still maisonettes. You know, the ones they've never quite got round to knocking down. It's not like a nice little cul-de-sac there, you know. No, no double gates. Nothing. There's no closing your matching blinds and shutting yourself off from reality there. Margy, you'd be lost.
MARGY	I live in a nice place. Like I don't even know about reality now.
SHARON	Not my reality you don't. My future, not even a house. A no-go zone. Living next door to Siobhan bleeding Walsh. That's my reality. What sort of life would that be for my kids, eh? Moving in next door to them.
LILY	Itchy.
SHARON	You're telling me. The whole block could do with a frigging good fumigate.
LILY	Frigging good evacuate.
SHARON	I know, yeah . . . Living there. Imagine it.
LILY	(*she dreads*) Yeah.

SHARON   That's if you can imagine it like. Where was it you lived as a kid, Marg? Oh, that's right. Yeah. Only you grew up, got a mortgage and got out.

MARGY   It wasn't like that.

SHARON   Wasn't it? I don't have no choice, Margy. Do what I can, when I can. If that means missing a dance for a ciggy run, it means missing a dance. Honest to God, it just goes to show. It doesn't take long does it. When hardship was just a distant memory. (*A pause*.) Oh yeah. And you want to know the real reason I come here, Marg. To forget. That's why. Forget all what there is I should really be thinking about. So go on, on your forms. Why don't you put that down as well. Them ones on the panel, you never know, they might be interested.

MARGY   Sharon. I didn't know.

          (SHARON *reaches for her drink, settles back*.)

SHARON   Some of us do have more to think about than just morris.

          (LILY *returns to her seat*.)

LILY   We do. More to think about than just filling in forms and hoping for the best.

MARGY   The best for the troupe.

LILY   You're the only one who's got time.

MARGY   Me? How old's your Jamie-Lee, seventeen?

LILY   Yeah, and she needs looking after. You know it all about kids now do you.

          (LILY *stands to move away*.)

LILY   Sharon. Ciggies.

SHARON   Twenty or a hundred. The hundred, works out the cheaper –

LILY   Twenty for now, will you.

                (SHARON *goes to the holdall.* LILY *calls after
                her.*)

LILY   And er, put it on my tab.

SHARON   Tab? What tab's this, Lil?

                (*Pause. An exchange of looks.* MARGY *is very
                used to this routine. She reaches her bag,
                takes out her purse.*)

MARGY   It's alright. I know. Rely on Margy.

LILY   I can't find my purse.

MARGY   Good old Margy.

LILY   I'll give it you back.

                (MARGY *goes to* SHARON, *she hands over the
                required cash.* SHARON *hands* LILY *the
                cigarettes, then returns to her position.*)

MARGY   I might not know much. But one of these days,
                I'd really love to see how you'd cope without
                me.

                (*Pause.*)

SHARON   Don't tell me. You're not thinking of leaving us
                are you, Marg?

LILY   No. Not again.

SHARON   'Cos if I had a pound for every time . . .

LILY   Laughing.

SHARON   I know. I would.

MARGY   Yeah? One day, I might just mean it though.
                Mightn't I?

LILY   (*quiet*) With a bit of bleeding luck.

(*Slight pause.* MARGY *walks away, she goes to the arena. Over the tannoy, an announcement is heard.*)

BIG JOAN   Troupe announcement. Could all troupe trainers please make their way to the tent. That's all troupe trainers to the tent please. The drawer for the order of dance is about to take place, thank you.

(LILY *returns to her seat. She takes off her jacket. She sits.*)

MARGY   It's alright, Lil. Don't worry yourself. I'll go.

(LILY *opens the cigarettes, lights one up. She smokes. She puts on* SHARON'S *novelty stetson, puts her feet up on a cool-box.* SHARON *sunbathes.*)

LILY   Well go on, Marg. In your own time.

(*After a moment,* MARGY *fetches the trophy. Surveying the scene, she stands alone. She clutches the trophy to her.*)

Scene Three

The encampment, a little later. From the tannoy, music plays: Hey Baby by DJ Otzi. LILY *stands at one end of the encampment.* DONNA *is beside her.* DONNA *is in her twenties, a neat brunette, she is casually dressed but well-groomed, her baby's pram is at her side.* LILY *is dressed as before. The championship trophy has been removed.*

Both LILY *and* DONNA *stare into the pram. The hood of the pram is up, a parasol shades the opening.*

DONNA   Then I just thought . . . Oh go on. Drive. Why not. Wales, it's not as far as you think. She screamed all the way like. But what can you do.

LILY   You can't do nothing.

Donna	No.
Lily	She is though, Don. Honest to God.
Donna	Aaah.

(Donna *fusses at the pram. She removes the pram's cover, the baby's shawl. She repositions the pram.*)

Lily	Absolutely gorgeous. I'm not messing Don . . . I have seen some babies in my time but her . . . I mean your mother told me she was like. Every time I go in to your shop, ever since you had her . . . Her hair, what she had on last night, what our Donna's putting on her tomorrow. She was the same when your gay Stephen was born. Every little fart described in glorious technicolour. But this one . . . no wonder you couldn't wait to bring her.
Donna	I just thought.
Lily	No. No bleeding wonder.
Donna	I wanted you all to see her. I just thought, everybody here.

(Lily *observes the baby.*)

Lily	Aaah. Don. Look at her.

(*Slight pause.*)

Donna	They are here, aren't they, Lil? The girls. Margy?
Lily	Oh aye. Margy. You know Margy. Never misses a trick. Sweet Jesus. Don. And here's me. I haven't even give her nothing.
Donna	Lily. You don't have to.

(Lily *looks about. She searches in her handbag.*)

LILY   No, sod that. My mam. She always used to do it. There must be hundreds of girls round this dancing arena brought up on my mam crossing their palm with fifty pence. It's tradition. Or luck. Or some other frigging thing. Oh, eh. Can I ever find my purse?

(LILY's *search is fruitless. Instead, she reaches for* MARGY'S *bag.*)

LILY   Margy. She can put it on my tab.

DONNA   Aaah.

(LILY *takes out the cash, a two pound coin. She hands over the cash.* DONNA *accepts.*)

LILY   No, go on. You take it. It won't hurt my finances any more than they already are.

DONNA   Aaah . . .

LILY   Babies, love. They're very expensive things. You've only got to look at that pram. That pram must have set you back a bit.

DONNA   My mum.

LILY   Was it yeah? Well, I suppose you've got to haven't you, these days. Your first, first grandchild for her.

DONNA   Everybody. They've all been really kind.

(LILY *takes up the baby's shawl. She fingers at it, impressed.*)

LILY   I'll say. And your fella?

DONNA   Ah yeah. You know.

LILY   Still with you?

DONNA   Moved in. Yeah.

LILY   Go 'way. God Donna, you must be. You must
                be made up with her.

                (DONNA *smiles*. LILY *indicates the arena. A
                troupe is dancing. She watches.*)

LILY   Eh. And one day. These little ones . . . That'll
                be her. Have you seen them? Look at her. This
                one, with the nappy swinging . . . This time
                next year, Don. I can just see her in a frilly little
                frock, can't you? Soon as she can walk, she'll
                be swinging her arms, marching her feet.

                (LILY *returns to the pram. She adjusts the
                shawl back into place.*)

LILY   Won't you. Eh? And alright babe, we might not
                have a tiny troupe like these but we've got
                better things lined up for you, haven't we?
                Mascot. I promise you. You can be our mascot
                any day. You mascot and your mother back in
                the troupe. What d'you think of that? Now
                that'd be something wouldn't it, eh Don?

                (DONNA *removes the shawl.*)

DONNA   It's better too cool than it is too hot. That's
                what the book says.

                (*She fusses at the pram once more. Off stage, a
                shout is heard.*)

SHARON   Lil . . . Lily.

                (SHARON *enters. Dressed as she was before, she
                carries a large holdall with her. Out of breath,
                she calls.*)

SHARON   Lil . . . you are never gonna fucking believe
                this.

LILY   Sha . . .

SHARON   Honest to God, the dirty bleeding bastards.

LILY   (*warningly*) Sharon.

SHARON	I'm not lying. Big Joan's tent. Just now. I goes in, right. You know, off load a few smokes. I thought cert, she's got the money, right . . . But anyway. When I got in there . . . (*She pauses.*) Wigan Pierettes. Only been reported by the Runcorn Parks and Gardens' for dumping shitty nappy bags behind their troupe bus last week. They're on a final warning.
LILY	Are they now? And so will you be if you're not bloody careful.
SHARON	What?
LILY	Visitors Sharon. D'you know what I mean?
	(SHARON *turns, seeing* DONNA *and the pram for the first time.*)
SHARON	Hiya. Don.
DONNA	Hiya.
SHARON	You alright?
LILY	She was till you showed up.
SHARON	Lily, all I'm doing is telling you what I seen. Friggin'ell. Shit and nits, welcome to the world.
LILY	For Jesus' sake.
DONNA	What is it?
SHARON	Shit and nits, love. Welcome to the morris.
DONNA	Who's got nits? Has somebody got nits?
	(*From her coolbox,* SHARON *breaks open a bottle, a Bacardi Breezer or similar. She drinks.*)
SHARON	'Cos Big Joan, right. You should have seen her. She was out of that saggy chair, pointing the

finger . . . she give her loads. You know her,
their trainer . . .

LILY

The one with the moustache.

SHARON

Her. They're a total disgrace. To themselves,
the Association . . . And the look on her face.
Down all her chins. It was like thunder. And
there was me, stood there. Honest to God, it
was brilliant. Just me and my duty free. Poor
Margy like, she missed the whole lot. As I was
going in, she was going out.

(SHARON *continues on with her bag.*)

LILY

Margy? In Big Joan's wigwam? What was she
doing in there?

SHARON

Taking the trophy back. Taking the drawer.

LILY

The order of dance. And?

SHARON

And what?

LILY

What number are we?

SHARON

Dunno. On the sell. I was steering well clear.
But you never know, Lil. Pierettes. They throw
a dirty Pampers today . . . It'll be one less
troupe for us to worry about.

(SHARON *offers a bottle in* DONNA'S *direction.*)

SHARON

Don? Chaser.

DONNA

No . . . Breast. You know.

SHARON

Is it yeah.

DONNA

Nits? Has somebody really got nits?

(*Readying to sunbathe,* SHARON *sets down her
bottle.* LILY *swipes the drink out of reach.*)

LILY

For frig's sake. Haven't you got nothing better
to do?

(LILY *indicates the pram. She then goes on to transfer the drink into a plastic glass – any leftovers she drinks for herself.*)

SHARON   Ah, yeah. Donna. What am I like. When you've got two of your own, that's what it is. You know, two little, God forgive me . . . But they are, honest to God, two little –

LILY   Swines.

SHARON   Swines. Yeah. Well you forget like. Other people actually like their kids.

           (SHARON *peers into the pram. Slight pause.*)

SHARON   So how was it then, Don. D'you have an easy time of it or what?

DONNA   It was alright. You know.

SHARON   What? Even the labour, like.

DONNA   Well . . .

SHARON   Hurts, doesn't it?

DONNA   God. Sometimes.

SHARON   I know yeah and then come the stitches. And d'you know what happened to me. Both times. They're down their doing their stuff and I'm screaming and the next minute like, they give me the baby to hold. I mean what's that supposed to do, take your mind off it?

DONNA   I don't know.

SHARON   Does it shite. It doesn't, does it.

DONNA   I don't know, I never had any stitches.

SHARON   Not one?

DONNA   No.

SHARON   Donna, what have you been doing?

LILY   Jesus. Knit one, bleeding pearl one, me.

SHARON   Me the same. Not a stitch . . . ?

DONNA   None. Even the midwife said. Mine. It was, erm
            . . . as natural a birth as you could get with an
            epidural. It was. You know, and once she was
            in my arms . . . like, you soon forget the worst,
            don't you.

SHARON   I never. My downstairs. Smelt like a wet dog
            for a good week and a half.

LILY   Sharon.

SHARON   And the leftovers Donna, what come out of me.

DONNA   No . . .

SHARON   Honest to God.

LILY   She doesn't want to know.

SHARON   You could. You could have cut it with a steak
            knife.

            (DONNA *reaches for the water bottle close by.
            She takes a gulp.*)

DONNA   My God . . . is that . . . alcoholic?

            (DONNA *winces.*)

SHARON   Oh my God.

LILY   If it is, love –

DONNA   Oh my God.

LILY   If it is. Only a bit.

            (DONNA *sniffs the bottle. There is no doubt.*)

LILY   It won't do her any harm. She'll sleep for you.

SHARON   White rum.

(DONNA *sets down the bottle.*)

DONNA   And I suppose you think that's funny do you?

LILY   Donna . . .

            (*She takes the brake off the pram and moves away.* LILY *thrusts the bottle in* SHARON'S *direction, she follows.*)

LILY   One swig. She'll be alright.

DONNA   D'you reckon?

LILY   Perhaps, not used to it. It just, you know, seemed more to you.

DONNA   What's mine is hers. D'you know what I mean?

LILY   Love. You're her mother, would you have it any other way? And I tell you what. All this feeding, she's doing you a favour on it. From where I'm standing, you have got your figure right back lovely. Hasn't she? Hasn't she, Sha?

SHARON   (*under her breath*) She fucking would.

DONNA   This top. It hides a multitude.

LILY   This top. Listen to her. How old is she?

DONNA   Three weeks, last Tuesday.

LILY   Three weeks. A million bleeding dollars. You could walk straight back into this troupe. Lined up, no one'd be able to tell the bloody difference.

DONNA   I couldn't.

LILY   No. But. If you did. What's the point a good dress going to waste, that's what I say.

            (*Pause.*)

LILY   I do still bring it you know. Your dress.

DONNA   Mine?

LILY   On the bus it is. Spare dressbag, your name
            still on it. You know, with all them special ones
            I take home. Sad isn't it. All the ones I dream
            about coming back, that's what they are. And
            every week . . . you know, just in case. (*She
            pauses.*) Mind you, it's only the same as you'll
            be with her. There'll be some dresses you'll
            always want to keep.

            (*From off, a call is heard.*)

MARGY   (*off*) Right. Order of dance. Who wants to hear it?

LILY   And then like, there'll be some that you don't.

            (MARGY *enters, dressed as before.*)

MARGY   Well, the bad news or the worse news?

DONNA   Hiya Marg.

MARGY   Donna. Love . . . what are you doing here?

            (MARGY *goes to* DONNA. *She embraces her.*)

LILY   Sitting here. That's what she's been doing.
            Waiting. The poor girl, some welcome this has
            been. (*She points – herself,* SHARON.) Me. Her.

MARGY   Thank God she knows what it's like then.
            There's always something to keep me busy
            isn't there, Don. And now . . .

            (DONNA *adjusts at the pram for* MARGY *to peer
            in.* MARGY *continues, she moves away.*)

MARGY   We've been drawn number five, Lily.

LILY   And what's wrong with that?

MARGY   Middle of the field, that's what's wrong with it.
            If we're not careful, these judges'll be saving
            their winning points till last.

LILY   So? They always do.

MARGY   So. Number six, Speke Jags. Unless we're
                perfect, they could walk it. So what I was
                thinking. Tactics. Make them nervous. Spot on,
                we have to be. Top to bloody bottom . . .
                Entrance, exit, uniform and performance.
                Shakers . . . Lily. We need to get a shift on.

                (MARGY *goes to the large military-looking
                sack – the shaker bag. She drags it open,
                begins to pull out shakers.*)

MARGY   Sharon.

SHARON   What?

MARGY   Fluff. Lil, will you.

                (MARGY *drops a pair of shakers to each of
                them.*)

SHARON   You're messing aren't you?

MARGY   Donna. You remember don't you?

                (MARGY *deposits shakers onto* DONNA'S *lap.
                She sits close by.* MARGY *begins to fluff the
                shakers, efficiently and at speed, the only one
                doing so. [NB:Fluffing up shakers is a process
                to make the shaker a more full and even shape.
                This is done by wetting the first three fingers
                of either hand then rubbing the polythene
                strands vigorously between them. This
                separates out the individual strands therefore
                achieving the desired effect. The appearance
                of shakers is taken into consideration in the
                overall 'Costume and Appearance' section of
                a Judge's marking]. A pause.*)

MARGY   Eh. Did Lily tell you . . . ? That's what I'm
                doing. I'm applying for a grant.

                (*Partaking in her task,* LILY *fluffs the centre of
                the shakers with as little effort as possible.
                She tosses them aside.*)

MARGY	Morris as a sport.
DONNA	Go 'way.
MARGY	You want to see it, Don. Talk about bureaucracy, it's worse than being in work. The paperwork. I'll show you after. I even had to take a half-day's holiday. But move with the times. You've got to. Like today. Stay one step ahead otherwise, you don't stand a chance.
DONNA	Great.
MARGY	I know yeah. So if our boat comes in. This lot. I might just hand over the cheque and leave them to it. (*She jokes.*) And don't you worry Don. Any spare places in this troupe. I'll make sure you're the first one to know.
SHARON	My God. Can't you the leave the girl alone? A new baby . . .
DONNA	I'm alright.
SHARON	That's her trouble you see.
DONNA	It's alright.
SHARON	No Donna. It's not. If she wants to come back Margy, it's up to her. Not no one else. Alright.
MARGY	It was just a thought.
SHARON	Yeah and that's what it can stay. Don't you ever learn? Life can be hard enough without having to morris dance and all. But you wouldn't understand that, would you? Not like the likes of us. We know how bad it gets. My kids. They've already had my fanny, my tits. What more do they want, d'you know what I mean? Dancing. It's the last thing a new mother needs to think about.
MARGY	Yeah, Sharon. You're right. Leader, it's the last thing anyone in their right mind needs to think

about. You know, between the workload and
the worrying and the losing sleep. I mean,
where's the rest of the troupe? They should be
over here. It's not like they don't know is it.
But you know. This shower. Where've they
scarpered now?

(MARGY *sits. She resumes fluffing once more.*)

MARGY   Not a dancer in sight. Where did I go wrong, eh?

(*A slight pause.*)

DONNA   You could always try looking over the fair,
             Marg. That's where they were before.

MARGY   The fair?

DONNA   I only cut through 'cos I thought she might like
             it, the lights and everything, but . . .

MARGY   Our girls?

DONNA   They were wearing your tracksuits.

LILY   Our Ladys'? Are you sure?

SHARON   Fuckin 'ell, Lily. She could hardly go wrong.

DONNA   A big gang of them. Aaah, and you could tell
             the lads they were with were on the pull and all.

LILY   Lads?

SHARON   Where there's lads, there's Our Lady All
             Angels'.

MARGY   I'll go.

LILY   Too right you'll go. And bring them back.

(MARGY *collects herself.* DONNA *smiles.*)

DONNA   Aaah, it didn't half take me back though. Soon
             as I saw them . . . And your Jamie-Lee. I had to
             laugh. How she didn't see me.

SHARON	Pushing a pram, love. You're invisible to the world.
DONNA	All over this lad she was. Sitting on his knee and that. God, I felt ashamed.
LILY	My Jamie-Lee?
DONNA	I mean don't get me wrong, I pretended not to notice.
LILY	What are you saying?
DONNA	Well. Sometimes, you can't help but look can you?
LILY	Now hang on a minute. That girl.
MARGY	Lily . . .
LILY	That girl is whiter than white.
DONNA	I wasn't saying –
LILY	I know what you was saying.
MARGY	Alright.
LILY	Alright? What's up with her eh? Back five minutes and causing bleeding trouble.
DONNA	No.
LILY	No? Why did you come here, eh? Eh?
	(DONNA *doesn't reply.*)
LILY	Going round, telling me that. She is my little girl.
	(LILY *grabs her jacket, stuffs cigarettes into her pocket.*)
MARGY	Are you going then, are you Lil?
LILY	'Course I'm frigging going.
MARGY	And the rest of them. I want them all. Over here.

LILY   Margy. Give it a rest.

                (LILY *exits. Pause.*)

DONNA   All I meant was. Jamie-Lee. That sort of thing.
                That used to be me.

                (MARGY *goes to the shaker bag, she removes
                more shakers. Returning to* DONNA, *she hands
                out a set to her. She turns to* SHARON. SHARON
                reaches her holdall, she stands.)

MARGY   And where d'you think you're going?

SHARON   No girls, no practise. What's the point? Eh,
                Don? You don't want a tracksuit, do you?

DONNA   No.

                (SHARON *exits. A pause.* MARGY *sits. She
                begins to fluff-up her shaker. Over the tannoy
                music begins to play: Tell Me Ma by Sham
                Rock.* MARGY *indicates the arena.*)

MARGY   So what's it like Don? Good to be back?

                (MARGY *observes, continuing her task.* DONNA
                *sits beside her. She makes no attempt at the
                shaker. She stares to the pram.*)

                              Scene Four

The encampment. Later, the same day.

Over the tannoy, music plays. In the centre of the encampment,
DONNA *sits alone. Eating take-away chips, she gazes out,
towards the arena. The pram is close by. On a seat beside her,
another portion of chips lies half-eaten.*

After a moment, JAMIE-LEE *enters.* JAMIE-LEE *is seventeen and
loves it. She wears a troupe tracksuit. Her long hair is loose
and pin-straight. She makes for the arena. She is followed by*
LILY, *dressed as before.* LILY *carries with her a polystyrene*

tray – the remnants of burger and fries. She picks at them as she speaks. LILY *and* JAMIE-LEE *are mid row.*

LILY   For Jesus' sake. How many times . . .?

JAMIE-LEE   I've told you.

LILY   All you've told me is a pack of lies. Behind
                some burger van. That's where she was,
                Donna.

JAMIE-LEE   Waiting for my food.

LILY   With a lad?

JAMIE-LEE   We were having a laugh.

LILY   And I want to know what you were doing.

JAMIE-LEE   My food. That I never got a chance to eat.

                (JAMIE-LEE *walks away. Over the tannoy an
                announcement is heard. Automatically they
                join in the applause.*)

BIG JOAN   A big thank you, Toxteth Debutantes. And that
                concludes our Junior Morris section. All girls
                for the marching comp on the arena, please . . .

                (LILY *continues as she claps.*)

LILY   D'you hear that Jamie? And you know what
                comes after a marching comp, don't you?
                Before you know it we'll be dancing. Only
                where are the girls, eh? I turned round and they
                were gone. 'Cos of you.

JAMIE-LEE   Mum. I've heard it.

                (JAMIE-LEE *goes to the pram. She peers in.*)

LILY   Yeah and so have I. Plenty of times. Our Lady
                All Angels', that's what's writ across your
                back. You want to be careful. Spoiling the name
                of this troupe.

(*Slight pause.*)

JAMIE-LEE   Aaah. Donna. Look at her . . . Hiya. God! The hair on her.

DONNA   Better than mine.

JAMIE-LEE   Aah. I bet she's perfect, isn't she?

DONNA   I think so.

LILY   (*she goes to the pram*) She might be now. That age so was she. Our Jamie-Lee, you could take her anywhere. A smile for everyone she had. But now . . . now it's the clothes, the mobile. And as for over there. Jesus wept.

JAMIE-LEE   Can't you just forget it. For once.

LILY   No. Jamie-Lee. I can't. 'Cos I mean it . . . the way you're carrying on today.

JAMIE-LEE   I am?

LILY   By that fair. Talk about parading it.

JAMIE-LEE   It wasn't just me. They were there and all, you know. What about the rest of them.

LILY   The rest of them aren't my girl.

(LILY *walks away. She sits, she eats.*)

JAMIE-LEE   They're your troupe though, aren't they. But I don't see you giving them grief in public. Totally ashamed. I don't see them getting dragged back over here.

LILY   Perhaps 'cos they wasn't the ones doing nothing wrong.

JAMIE-LEE   Mum. Neither was I.

(LILY *sets down her food.*)

LILY   Donna saw you. And the baby. She saw you.
                (*Slight pause.*) With a lad. On his knee. Like
                some kind of slut.

JAMIE-LEE   Like what?

LILY   You heard.

DONNA   I never said slut. All over him, I said.

LILY   What ever you said. It's all means the same to
                me, love.

JAMIE-LEE   Ta, Donna. Thanks a lot.

LILY   I'm telling you, it'll be plaits for you today girl.

JAMIE-LEE   (*she gestures her hair*) Plaits. Behave. I was up
                at half-six ironing this.

                (*Pause.*)

LILY   Some woollyback. I thought you of all people
                could have picked someone better than that.

JAMIE-LEE   Better than what?

LILY   I only wish I'd managed to get a closer look.
                But he was soon skulking off, wasn't he? Him
                and his mates when I come on the scene . . .
                What was he like, Jamie-Lee? Drinking cider
                was he. And talking funny. And earrings.

JAMIE-LEE   (*reiterating* LILY) 'One earring, they're gay.
                Two, they're a girl'.

LILY   That's right. Some bleeding no-mark. And you
                have to go and fall for it.

JAMIE-LEE   Some no-mark . . . ? What gives you the right?

LILY   Every right. You was in a pram yourself once
                you know. And who was pushing it? But that's
                the trouble with kids. All what you have ever
                done for them. Wiped your nose, wiped your
                arse.

JAMIE-LEE	Mum.
LILY	If it wasn't for me, Jamie-Lee. Where would you be now? Eh? Tell me that one.
JAMIE-LEE	No-mark. He is my fella. (*She pauses.*) You heard.

(JAMIE-LEE *goes to the large check bag. She brings out her pumps.*)

LILY	Your fella. Since when, half-ten this morning? Will you talk sense.
JAMIE-LEE	I'm seventeen, mum.
LILY	Not to me you're not.
JAMIE-LEE	Well I am to him. I am. He wanted to see me. So . . . He drived over all that way, him and his mates. Just to see me. From round by ours, all that way. My fella. Alright.

(*Slight pause.*)

LILY	He's got a bloody car?
JAMIE-LEE	He's twenty-two.
LILY	God bless us almighty . . .
JAMIE-LEE	Come on. He's hardly gonna be twelve, is he?
DONNA	Is he? Really.
JAMIE-LEE	Donna. What's it got to do with you, eh?
DONNA	Twenty-two. You'll have to be careful.
LILY	Too right she'll have to be careful.
JAMIE-LEE	Don't start. On that.
DONNA	No. 'Cos some of the girls I know . . . You know, the likes of Sharon and that, the way they end up, Jamie-Lee. On their own, a few

kids, in some flat somewhere . . . It's all down to fellas. Fellas and a few drinks.

JAMIE-LEE   Well it won't be me.

LILY   Twenty-bleeding-two.

DONNA   Next thing Jamie, he'll be asking you to move in with him.

JAMIE-LEE   He can ask what he likes. The answer'd still be no. No way, I'm at college. I want more out of my life. Kids can wait. And so can he. That's how serious he is over me. Or he was. Before you come shouting. Till they had to call security.

LILY   Jamie-Lee. You're still only a baby.

JAMIE-LEE   I was with a lad, mum. So what? You never had to go making a show and shouting your mouth, bringing Siobhan Walsh's nits into it . . . But you never think about that, do you? Something to laugh at. Our troupe. That's all I am to them. Trainer's daughter, always treated different.

LILY   Only 'cos you are different. You are.

JAMIE-LEE   Donna. Give us a chip, will you?

LILY   Now, eh. Jamie . . . You have got to dance yet.

DONNA   Honest to God. Siobhan Walsh. Has she really got nits?

             (JAMIE-LEE *moves away. She begins to whiten her pumps. Over the tannoy, troupe music starts to play. On the arena, the marching competition is in progress. After a moment,* DONNA *stands, she moves the pram away from the chairs. Pause.*)

LILY   My poor mam . . . What she'll make of all this, God help her. She'll be doing the kick-out step in her grave. You and your acting up. It won't do her a bit of good. Your nan, Jamie-Lee. 'Cos she might have been a lot of things your Nan but she was proud of you. Wasn't she? Proud. When your photo was in the Merseymart. Mascot of the Year 1994. There wasn't a pensioner she'd let pass and that picture, it'd be out of her handbag, all ringlets and medals. And smiles . . . How times change. (*She pauses.*) Time was, you would have been falling over yourself to get in this marching competition.

JAMIE-LEE   Would I?

LILY   And you would have won it and all. She'd only have to go up on her toes, wouldn't she Don, and the medal was hers. Every marching competition she ever went in for.

JAMIE-LEE   Every one you put me in for.

DONNA   Well she deffo would have won this one. (*Indicating the arena.*) Margy's judging it.

LILY   She is what?

DONNA   Margy. On the arena. Haven't you seen?

(LILY *observes the arena. She moves closer.*)

LILY   Of all the bloody cheek! How did she wangle that one?

DONNA   (*returning, she sits*) No, Lil. What happened was . . .

LILY   I know what happened. In that tent, her and Big Joan. A good old talk she's had.

DONNA   No. Before right. We were having our dinner and the next thing . . .

LILY   This form you see. It's gone to her head.

DONNA   Lily, no. No girls here, Margy was worried sick.
             I mean, what else could she do? Big Joan, you
             can't just say no.

LILY   Can't you? When she should be over here,
             rounding up her own troupe.

DONNA   That's what she thought you was doing.

LILY   Donna . . . What have I told you? You don't
             know nothing. Alright.

             (LILY *walks away. She lights up a cigarette.*)

LILY   Who does she think she is, eh? Look at her . . .

             (LILY *smokes close to the pram. She watches
             the arena. She begins to push at the pram,
             back and forth.*)

LILY   The way she's looking at that kid . . . Jesus.
             They're only age ten. It's a bit of fun, not
             Supreme Dancer of the Year finale, d'you know
             what I mean?

             (DONNA *goes to the pram, she intervenes. She
             moves the pram away, this time to the far end
             of the encampment.* LILY *continues.*)

LILY   Have you seen this? Jamie-Lee . . . the way
             she's looking. I can hardly bear to . . . where's
             she going now? . . . Jamie. She is. She's going
             to Big Joan. I knew it. See? Talking to her.
             See . . .

             (JAMIE-LEE *stands to watch the arena.*)

LILY   Talk about being in on it.

JAMIE-LEE   She's pointing dancers. They're deciding the
             winner.

LILY   Deciding something.

JAMIE-LEE   Mum, it's a marchie. Anyone can judge a
             marchie.

LILY	I never have.
JAMIE-LEE	You know what I mean.
LILY	I have never even been asked. All these years. Mind you, not that I've ever put myself forward, like. It's just not in my nature. Not like her.
	(JAMIE-LEE *returns to her place, resumes at her pumps.*)
JAMIE-LEE	(*with irony*) You want to watch her. Next thing, Grand Parade, she'll be on the top table giving out the medals.
LILY	I'm telling you, Jamie-Lee. If she can do it –
JAMIE-LEE	If she can do what?
LILY	You're gonna have to start bucking your ideas up, girl.
	(*A pause. The baby starts to cry.*)
LILY	Trust you. When the whole morris world is at your feet.
JAMIE-LEE	I'm sorry?
	(DONNA *pushes at the pram. The baby continues to cry.*)
LILY	She alright there, is she Don? Not hungry or anything? Too many distractions, that's your trouble.
JAMIE-LEE	Distractions. You mean lads.
LILY	Not thirsty? She doesn't sound too happy. Does she? Eh?
	(DONNA *doesn't reply.*)
LILY	Honest to God. You could have worked it out bloody better than this.

JAMIE-LEE   Worked out what?

LILY   A matter of time, Jamie-Lee. That's all it is. And
             all that you have ever wanted. Don't you start
             throwing it away now . . .

             (MARGY *enters from the arena. Dressed as
             before, she also wears her waistcoat. After a
             moment, the baby's cries start to fade.*)

MARGY   Did you see that? My God, the things you do
             for a favour. I thought it was never gonna end.
             I was starting to have visions, my whole life
             passing before my very eyes.

LILY   What like? All the competitions I have ever
             danced.

MARGY   It was. Morris, shakers, morris . . .

LILY   Big Joan.

MARGY   And that little Dinkie, that one of
             Sovereignettes. See, it's kids like her. Funding
             for morris, it should go without question. How
             she marched for the whole, entire . . . The
             stamina. Right up, on her toes. Unbelievable
             she is. Did you see her, Don?

DONNA   Aaah. Yeah.

MARGY   The little size of her.

JAMIE-LEE   She was brilliant.

MARGY   Did you see her, Lil?

LILY   No.

MARGY   Ah, you should. Arm work spot in, knees up
             here . . . Bloody'ell, listen to me.

             (MARGY *removes her waistcoat, she fetches
             some pumps.*)

MARGY	Right then. Pumps then practise. (*A pause.*) Our girls, they all back on the bus now, are they Lil?
LILY	Our girls? Like you care. No, you'd rather be off judging a marchie.
MARGY	Lily. She asked me. What else could I say?
LILY	No? You have got a troupe to practise.
MARGY	A troupe with no girls. All I was trying to do was keep in, score us some brownie points.
LILY	Trying to impress, more like.
MARGY	Well. Perhaps you better start getting used to it then. (*She pauses.*) Big Joan. She's just asked me. Well, more like whispered it really. Confidentiality, I suppose. You know, like the results. All hush-hush.
LILY	Asked you what?
MARGY	Big Joan. She's asked me to become an official adjudicator.
	(*Slight pause.*)
DONNA	Margy . . .
JAMIE-LEE	Oh my God.
MARGY	I know yeah. Middle of the arena.
LILY	An official what?
MARGY	It was as much a surprise to me.
LILY	Say it again.
JAMIE-LEE	A judge.
MARGY	A proper judge. Judging. Proper competitions.
LILY	You?

MARGY	She's asked me to be a judge.
LILY	You can frig off . . . She asked you?
MARGY	Just now.

(LILY *reaches for her jacket.*)

LILY	Cheeky fat bitch. My leader. Wait till I get hold of her.
JAMIE-LEE	Mum . . .
LILY	I hope you told her, Margy.
JAMIE-LEE	Mum. Leave it.
LILY	'Cos if you never, I will. Poaching girls that aren't hers to poach. You haven't even left and so far, you have got no frigging intention. What did she say to that, eh?
MARGY	She said . . . none of us can morris dance forever.

(LILY *pauses.*)

LILY	You're going to do it?
MARGY	I said I'm interested.
LILY	Said you're what?
MARGY	She wants me to start next season.

(LILY *goes to the chairs. She removes her jacket, she sits. Automatically,* DONNA *offers out the water bottle of alcohol to her.*)

| MARGY | Well. Big Joan really wants me on board. (*Pause.*) At least . . . if I say yes. It's not like I'd be leaving properly is it. Judging. Okay, I wouldn't be dancing, but . . . I could still come out with you, on the bus. There'd be nothing to stop me doing that. I could still help you train. Just . . . I'd be looking at it from the association's point of view. That's what Big |

Joan does. You know. For Speke.
Masterclasses. Imagine that, eh. A masterclass
for Our Ladys'. There wouldn't be no one who
could beat us then, would there? (*She pauses.*)
If Big Joan can do it. Why can't I?

LILY   Margy. 'Cos you can't, alright.

MARGY   Lily...

              (LILY *picks up the half-eaten portion of chips
              close by.*)

LILY   Who's are these? These going spare or what?

              (*A pause.* MARGY *returns to the pumps,
              emptying out the bag – its contents of
              footwear are paired together by elastic bands.
              There also a few single pumps, spares.*)

JAMIE-LEE   I think it's great, Marg. I'm really made up for
              you.

LILY   You? You are having me on?

JAMIE-LEE   Moving on. What's wrong with that?

LILY   She's a girl from Our Ladys', Jamie. Now all of
              a sudden, that's it, she wants to be a judge.

JAMIE-LEE   You wouldn't say nothing about no one else
              doing it though, would you. Any other troupe.
              It's alright for the likes of them. But for us...

MARGY   Jamie.

LILY   She's one of my girls. She's leaving us behind.

JAMIE-LEE   Your girls? Like we're all here for your
              convenience.

LILY   I can see it all now. On there, strutting round
              that field. Scribbling. Nodding your head.
              Yeah. Till the next minute you see a shaker
              mistake and that'll be it. Down your nose like
              we're a piece of dirt.

MARGY   Come on Lily. I haven't even decided yet.

LILY   I'm telling you. With her on there. Simon
               frigging Cowell. She will tear this troupe apart.

               (MARGY *pauses her task.*)

MARGY   You know what? And here's me thinking
               there'd be a little part of you that might be
               happy. Friends in high places. At last. 'Cos
               let's face it, you've moaned enough. Who's in
               with Big Joan, who's not. Who's got
               sponsorship. Why wasn't it us, Margy . . . ?

JAMIE-LEE   Speke Jags, it always is.

MARGY   Perhaps if you'd been a bit more go-getting
               yourself.

LILY   So that's what you call it, is it? Go-getting? I
               call it worming your way in.

MARGY   You would.

LILY   I'm not stupid, Margy. Her wigwam, a nice
               chat. This is what you were plotting, is it?

MARGY   I never had a clue. Minding my own business, I
               was eating my chips . . .

               (*Hearing this,* LILY *pauses eating.*)

MARGY   . . . the next thing, Big Joan come over here.

LILY   She come over here?

MARGY   Yeah. She stood there and she asked me to
               judge the marchie. Everything else, I knew
               nothing.

LILY   Big Joan? When I wasn't here? What's her
               game, eh? While I was gone looking for her.

JAMIE-LEE   Oh, great.

LILY   Someone could have bleeding told me.

DONNA   I did.

LILY   No one tells me nothing.

DONNA   I did try.

LILY   See. Jamie-Lee. If you'd have behaved
            yourself. All this.

            (*Pause.* LILY *moves away.*)

LILY   She's always had it in for me, her. My leader
            for her judge. Not like she's ever asked me like.
            No, not Lily. All my years experience and not
            even asked so much as to judge best decorated
            bleeding bus. But that's Big Joan all over. Pure
            jealous. She can't bear talent, her.

DONNA   No wonder you hate her, Lily.

LILY   No bloody wonder I do now.

            (*Slight pause.*)

JAMIE-LEE   Aah, yeah. Junior Leader of the Year. How old
            were you mum? Thirteen. And a half. (*She
            smiles.*) Big Joan beat her by one point so she
            ragged her hair out.

LILY   Alright. I was a kid, alright.

JAMIE-LEE   On the Moonwalk.

LILY   She hit me first.

JAMIE-LEE   You always say that.

LILY   I had a slap mark. Your Nan nearly had to lodge
            a complaint. Big Joan she was a right little
            bitch. I should have bloody known then. She
            always has to go and spoil it all.

(A pause.)

MARGY   Come on, Lil. We've got to dance yet. Finish these and a good practise. If we really put them through their paces, Lil. Me and you.

LILY   Me and you?

MARGY   Our girls . . .

(LILY walks away. She sits.)

MARGY   You did find our girls, didn't you?

JAMIE-LEE   Find them? It's a wonder you never heard her from here.

MARGY   Well. Where are they? Are they coming over or what?

JAMIE-LEE   Or what.

(As usual, MARGY springs into action. She reaches her mobile, begins to text.)

MARGY   Right . . . who's got a phone? Which girl.

JAMIE-LEE   Everyone.

MARGY   Who's got credit? Which one has got credit?

(There is no reply. The baby begins to cry. DONNA sighs. At the pram, she pushes at it once more.)

MARGY   You know . . . there is still a dance to sort out, you know.

(LILY puts her feet up on a cool-box. She relaxes. DONNA pushes at the pram. The baby continues to cry. A pause. On her phone, MARGY begins to text once more. Lights fade.)

ACT TWO

Scene One

The encampment. The same day, slightly later.

Before the chairs, a dozen perfectly whitened pumps are lined up in pairs. Some are unlaced, some laced, ready to wear, with ribbon and bells. Over the tannoy, music plays: Can't Get You Out Of My Head by Kylie Minogue.

In the centre of the encampment is SHARON. *Changing into her uniform, she steps into her dress over her clothes. Her bottle of alcohol, now refilled, stands on the cool-box.* JAMIE-LEE *sits a distance away. Now wearing her morris dress, she puts on her socks, brushes her hair, etc. Close to her, the baby's pram is positioned.* SHARON *watches the arena as she changes. A troupe is dancing. Still in full uniform,* MARGY *stands beside her. She is keen to speak.*

SHARON	The poor girl. It doesn't look like she's lost anything to me.
MARGY	Sharon.
SHARON	She can hardly cross her feet. Not a bleeding ounce, girl. Look at her.
MARGY	(*interjecting*) Sharon. Hang on a minute.
SHARON	That's the only reason why she still comes you know. Weight Watchers.
MARGY	Sharon. I need to know.
SHARON	She told me. The other week. I was in the toilets right, like that. Waiting for ages. And this cubicle opens.
MARGY	Will you tell me. What did you see?
SHARON	Her. The tears were streaming.
MARGY	Just now. Classique.

SHARON	They were by the buses.
MARGY	But what was it you saw?
SHARON	Classique.
MARGY	Yeah.
SHARON	Classique. Like I told you. (*She pauses.*) I come here for a day out you know, Margy. I've told you. Classique. By the buses. What else do you want? Blood?
MARGY	No. I don't want us to go on there and embarrass ourselves like what your poor mate does, every week.
SHARON	Fat Welsh Sarah. She's not my mate.
MARGY	I need to know.

(*Slight pause.*)

SHARON	I was at this bus right . . . Milano's or Sovereignettes or . . . they all look the same to me. But I was there right. At this bus with my ciggies out. Two-fifty a packet, five for a tenner . . .
MARGY	Yeah.
SHARON	Yeah. Then I heard the music.
MARGY	Our music.
SHARON	Last season's. Well, I hears Tragedy the Remix and I looks, don't I? And there they was. That's all. What I told you. Classique was practising to our music. Marg.

(SHARON *turns for* MARGY *to do up her zip.*)

MARGY	Honest to God. It gets on my nerves. Season after season, crap troupes thinking they can go

round pinching what they like. Your dress
design one minute, colour of your shakers the
next.

SHARON   It's a free country, Marg.

MARGY   It might well be. But this. Our last season's
music. Haven't they got a mind of their own?

SHARON   Didn't look like it. Not from where I was
standing. 'Cos like, thinking about it, it might
not have been just the music . . . I've got a
feeling they was doing our turn-about move
and all.

MARGY   Our move.

SHARON   They was going up-up-around.

MARGY   Our turn-about?

SHARON   I was finishing my Breezer, but I think . . .

MARGY   They were doing our turn-about move?

SHARON   Same arms. Yeah . . . Same turn.

MARGY   I do not believe this. No girls, no practise. It's
the last thing we bloody need. We're going to
have to have a whole new move.

SHARON   Now?

JAMIE-LEE A whole new move.

SHARON   You mean, learn it?

MARGY   Now think. What is it. Staggered lines, isn't it.
Into the turn-about . . .

           (*From her handbag,* MARGY *takes out a
           notebook and pen. She concentrates. In full
           view,* SHARON *puts on her frilly over-knickers.*)

SHARON   Marg. Come on. Can't you just look on the
bright side for once. Another troupe ripping off
our move. We must be doing something right.

MARGY   That's exactly what I am doing. They're
               dancing before us. By the time we get on there,
               the cheeky gets, who'll look like the sly
               copycats then?

SHARON   (*she hesitates*) Them?

MARGY   Us. I mean it, soon as the Senior section's
               finished. An official complaint.

SHARON   Alright, Marg. Just 'cos you're going up in the
               world.

MARGY   Sharon, my situation has got nothing to do
               with it. This isn't points, this is principle.

SHARON   Is it yeah?

               (MARGY *glances the arena.*)

MARGY   Oh my God. Sovereignettes. Have they nearly
               finished?

SHARON/   Yeah.
JAMIE-LEE

               (JAMIE-LEE *stands. She checks in the pram then
               goes to the pumps. Searching for her pair, she
               checks along the row.*)

MARGY   Back into bloody marching. Number eight . . .
               Opposite partner, five. No. If she goes there
               . . . where is Lily when you need her?

SHARON   The beer tent.

MARGY   Alright. Sha. Don't make things worse than
               they already are.

SHARON   I'm not. Being a trainer, it's a very stressful
               job.

MARGY   Really?

SHARON   It is when you might have just lost your right
            hand it is. If you might be leaving, Margy. You
            know, drowning her sorrows with the longest
            half of lager in the world. You can hardly blame
            her.

MARGY   Yeah well. Any excuse to get down the beer
            tent.

            (*From the tannoy an announcement is heard.*)

BIG JOAN   A big thank you to the first troupe in our
            Senior Section, Sovereignettes.

            (*Automatically, they applaud.*)

JAMIE-LEE   You never know, Marg. My mum reckons she
            makes up her best routines in beer tents.

MARGY   On the back of ciggy packets, yeah. No. If
            number ten turns. Then . . . this doesn't bloody
            work out. My God. How long have we got? I
            can't even think.

            (*From the tannoy an announcement is heard.*)

BIG JOAN   Thank you Sovereignettes. Next on the arena.
            Classique.

MARGY   Classique?

SHARON   Classique. Margy.

JAMIE-LEE   Our turn-about?

MARGY   This I do not want to see.

            (MARGY *moves away. Troupe music begins to
            play.*)

SHARON   Eh. At least Sovereign had a shit dance.

JAMIE-LEE   Yeah. One dance nearer to going home, thank
            God.

MARGY	This is our big chance. This dance . . . I wanted this to be perfect.
SHARON	We will be.
JAMIE-LEE	'Course we will.

(SHARON *drinks*. JAMIE-LEE *continues rocking the pram from where she lies.* MARGY *throws down her book.*)

MARGY	Right. Well come on then. If you're so confident.
SHARON	You what?
MARGY	On your feet. It's the best way.

(MARGY *pulls* SHARON *to her feet. She guides her into position.*)

SHARON	My ale . . .
MARGY	Number eight. Jamie-Lee. It's sort of the turn-about, right. Based on the turn-about only . . .
SHARON	It's not.
MARGY	Jamie . . .
JAMIE-LEE	Do I have to?
MARGY	I need to work this out. On my feet.
JAMIE-LEE	So what difference will I make?
MARGY	Number five.
JAMIE-LEE	My mum's not here. Will you give us a break?
MARGY	Do I look like I'm having a break?
JAMIE-LEE	I'm supposed to be looking after the baby.

MARGY	What is up with you? (*Slight pause.*) True love, is it. You'll soon be over him, Jamie-Lee. Every boyfriend I had, three months.
JAMIE-LEE	I don't think so.
SHARON	Three months.
MARGY	Fellas and morris. Believe me.
SHARON	Doesn't say much for your fella, Margy.
MARGY	Well it should. My fella was the only one who could put up with it.
SHARON	Not any more. The poor sod mightn't have to. God . . . Margy, no more morris. How will you cope?
MARGY	How will I cope?
SHARON	We'll be alright. Me in your place. I could be leader.
MARGY	You must be joking.
SHARON	What d'you reckon? 'Ere y'are, Marg. Give us a go.
MARGY	Sharon. A leader's got to be serious.
SHARON	I am serious. If you leave someone's got to take over.

(MARGY *consults at her book.*)

MARGY	Right. What it is. From the staggered lines, the three-lines-of-four. If we go into a sort of two spread out two-groups-of-four, two at either end. The same arm-movements . . . but with like the side diamonds different. And a turn. One way, at an angle, with all of us . . . Then straight out carrying on into the old routine, into marching and off. If we can work that one out, it'll be diferent, d'you see what I mean? D'you know what I'm saying.

SHARON   The two spread out what?

MARGY   Like. Diamonds.

(MARGY *stands in a central position to explain.*)

MARGY   Well. Me here. Leader. One two-groups-of-four either side. Eleven and twelve at the top, one and two facing me.

SHARON   Facing you. Which way?

MARGY   This way.

SHARON   On the arena as well. Are you facing that way?

MARGY   This way. I'm facing . . . I'm here. Right?

SHARON   Right. You're there. So what number does that mean I am?

MARGY   Eight. You're Siobhan.

SHARON   Siobhan. Why do I have to be Siobhan?

MARGY   'Cos she's number eight.

SHARON   What are you saying?

MARGY   I'm not saying nothing.

SHARON   The likes of you . . . That's right. Just lump us all together.

MARGY   All I'm saying, I need number eight.

SHARON   Nitty Walsh. I would be her. I might be hard-up but I'm bleeding clean.

MARGY   If I can just work this out from the staggered lines.

SHARON   You cheeky bitch.

MARGY   Sharon. It doesn't matter what number you are, alright. Who you are . . .

SHARON   Good. 'Cos my real number, I'm number ten.

MARGY   Well, eight first. Then. When the rest of them's ready. Then you can learn your own place as well.

SHARON   As well? Oh frig me.

          (SHARON *unzips her dress, loosens it. She drinks.* MARGY *studies her book for a moment.*)

MARGY   Alright. We're here. Jamie. Number five.

SHARON   Over there.

MARGY   She should be over here.

SHARON   Number five? Are you sure?

MARGY   Sharon, it's a move. How we get into it, the arm-work. All I want is the effect.

SHARON   With bleeding two of us?

MARGY   Sharon.

SHARON   The full effect. That's what we need.

          (SHARON *goes to the pram. She wheels it away.* JAMIE-LEE *stands to intervene.*)

JAMIE-LEE Eh! I was minding her.

SHARON   She's asleep.

JAMIE-LEE If Donna comes back. Donna's only gone to express you know.

SHARON   Oh yeah. What is it . . . To build up enough so she can leave the baby for the first time like ever. Jamie-Lee . . .

JAMIE-LEE   It's her baby.

                 (*In the centre,* SHARON *positions the pram.*)

SHARON   Whatever happened to a bottle, like. I mean, I
                 wasn't breastfed and I'm alright. These modern
                 mums and their tits. In the centre, Marg? She
                 can be leader.

MARGY   Just here.

SHARON   That's it.

                 (MARGY *manoeuvres* JAMIE-LEE *away from the
                 pram.* SHARON *passes out shakers.*)

MARGY   Jamie-Lee. If you can just . . .

JAMIE-LEE   Margy. Don't you leave her side she told me.

SHARON   She never bleeding meant it. Get hold.

MARGY   If we can just get this done. For one minute.

SHARON   I hope it is. I've still got my smokes target to
                 hit. I worked it out. Two hundred a day, I tick
                 over just nice.

                 (MARGY *takes up a place. Facing forward,
                 they are all positioned equally around the
                 pram.*)

MARGY   Here we go then. Her leader. Me number two.
                 From the lines, straight out, move to there. Into
                 the diamonds. You got it?

SHARON   Got it.

MARGY   Marking it through. We ready?

                 (MARGY *begins practise step. The others join
                 in. Ready to begin the move,* MARGY *raises her
                 hands to her shoulders. The others follow.*)

MARGY   Okay. And . . .

(Their arm-movements begin. They perform the move. They move out into another position, MARGY talks the move through.)

MARGY   Move. Two. Three. Four.

(LILY enters. She watches the move. Over her shoulder, SHARON makes constant checks on her performance.)

MARGY   Five. Six. Turn. Turn one.

(MARGY turns. Seeing LILY for the first time, she pauses.)

MARGY   Lily . . .

LILY   Well. What do you call this, eh?

MARGY   Lil . . .

LILY   A new move?

MARGY   Have you heard about Classique?

LILY   I'm the trainer, Margy.

JAMIE-LEE   Mum. Don't start.

LILY   You keep out of it. This is between me and her.

MARGY   They pinched our move, Lil.

LILY   Bleeding meddling. Things what aren't bleeding yours.

(LILY grabs MARGY's shakers from her.)

MARGY   I'm saving your skin.

LILY   Behind my back?

MARGY   If you'd had been here.

LILY   That's right. Here we go.

Sharon	If you'd have been here, we wouldn't have bothered.
Margy	But you would have expected me to all the same.
Lily	My troupe. I don't think so.
Margy	Your troupe what I train.
Lily	You train?
Margy	I train, I practise. I teach.
Lily	You. You just walk all over.

(Lily *throws down the shakers*.)

Margy	Do I?
Sharon	Alright girls.
Margy	Without me. This troupe.
Lily	Not your troupe.
Margy	It always has been.
Lily	Not any more.
Sharon	(*throwing down her shakers*) I said. Ladies.

(*At that moment,* Donna *enters. She carries with her a baby's bottle-holder. She pauses.*)

Lily	You've left, haven't you, Marg.
Margy	And isn't that just what you wanted.
Lily	That's right.
Margy	Go on. Spit it out.
Sharon	Will you split it up.

DONNA   What is going on? Her . . . I told you to keep an
               eye on her.

JAMIE-LEE   I was.

DONNA   In full sun? I don't think so.

MARGY   Donna . . .

DONNA   Using her.

LILY   Don't look at me. It's got nothing to do with
               me. (LILY *takes up her cigarettes.*
               Surreptitiously, she reaches for her purse.) If
               anyone wants me. Don't come and find me,
               alright.

               (LILY *exits. Slight pause.*)

MARGY   We weren't using her. Donna. This is an
               emergency.

               (DONNA *goes to the pram, she checks over the*
               baby.)

DONNA   I remember when you used to treat other
               peoples' kids like that. Someone's niece or
               something they just happened to bring along.
               It never mattered how little they were, just
               strap them in the buggy. A girl short, 'ere
               y'are, stick them in the middle.

               (DONNA *pushes the pram away.*)

SHARON   Has anyone got an headache tablet?

MARGY   Donna. It wasn't like that.

DONNA   Wasn't it?

JAMIE-LEE   Margy's got a big panic on. She wants a new
               move.

MARGY   Only because of Classique . . . Do you know
               what they've gone and done?

DONNA   And there's me. All that hard work just to keep up supply. Thinking no formula, I'm doing her good. Why I put myself through it. And it hurts . . . I was there and she was here . . . And you, you weren't even looking after her.

MARGY   We were.

DONNA   Leave it, Margy, you don't understand. Does she, Sha? Till you've got one of your own.

SHARON   Anyone got any Anadin? My head's done in.

DONNA   It's okay, babe. Mummy's here now, babe.

SHARON   I won't be long.

MARGY   Not now Sharon.

SHARON   I won't be long.

                 (SHARON *takes up her bag, she exits. Pause.*)

JAMIE-LEE   She is alright though, isn't she Don?

DONNA   She is. She's alright.

JAMIE-LEE   I would have let anyone run away with her . . . And it's not like Siobhan's here.

MARGY   She never come to no harm. Donna. We wouldn't have let her.

DONNA   It's not about her though, is it. (*A pause.*) It's just really hard.

MARGY   Well . . . Do you want to like, talk about it now Don, or . . .

DONNA   No, I'm alright. I am . . . It's just . . .

MARGY   Calm down a bit, we'll get this move gone.

DONNA   I'm sorry. I shouldn't even have said.

MARGY   No. 'Course you should. You're amongst
               friends.

DONNA   Only it might sound stupid. But . . .

               (*A pause.*)

DONNA   Before I had her. I just never realised . . . you
               know. I thought. Like, when I've got a little one
               . . . Everything. My whole life, and every day. I
               thought I'd you know . . . and not that I don't
               love her or anything . . . but that's how it's
               supposed to be, isn't it. You have a baby 'cos
               that's like what you do. And once you've had
               it. It's all lovely and baby and . . . the very first
               day I was at home with her. At home. On my
               own. It was just me and her. Her in the Moses
               basket in the living room and me on the chair.
               And I just sat there. Staring at her. For ages.
               Staring but, to go near her. I didn't even dare.
               Not like, in case I woke her up or anything. Just
               . . . and all morning, he kept phoning up from
               work. How is she, is she asleep, has she fed?
               And then in the afternoon, he went and phoned
               again. And I said to him, I'd just been the
               toilet. And he went, 'Have you?'. You know,
               like it was a shock. 'Have you? And was she
               alright?'. Like I wasn't meant to or something
               . . . and it was then. A split second. I knew.
               That's how hard it was. Just to leave her. Even
               just for a minute, to go to the toilet. For me. To
               go anywhere. Would she be alright? Would
               she be alright without me? And since then like.
               Even making a cup of tea. I time myself. See if I
               can stay in the kitchen, just that little bit
               longer, stay away from her a little bit more. Like
               I'm tormenting myself. I express where I can't
               see her, see if the milk still comes and in the
               night . . . Don't reach out till she cries. And if
               she looks at me, don't look at her till she looks
               away from me first. Just to see . . . It's only
               'cos I love her. Me without her, that's what it
               is. (*She pauses*). Sometimes I can't help but
               think. How was everything. How was it before?

MARGY   Is that why you come, Don?

DONNA   I don't know. I don't feel like I was ever a
               dancer now.

               (DONNA *wipes at her eyes.*)

DONNA   You think I'm mad now, don't you.

MARGY   Don't be soft.

DONNA   God . . . am I putting you off having kids or
               what?

MARGY   If I thought it was that easy, don't you think I
               would have done it by now?

DONNA   Yeah. Well that's what I mean.

               (MARGY *moves away, she consults at her
               book.*)

DONNA   Go on Margy. You can tell us.

MARGY   Tell you what?

DONNA   What else would you be thinking of packing in
               for, eh?

MARGY   I've been asked to join the association, I'm not
               packing in.

DONNA   Yeah but. Judging. It's not like dancing, is it?
               You can still judge. As long as it doesn't get in
               the way of the baby, like.

JAMIE-LEE   What baby's this?

MARGY   Donna . . . what baby? I'm not having a baby.

DONNA   Oh come on. You're leaving, aren't you.

MARGY   Donna. There is other things apart from kids
               you know.

DONNA	Like what?
MARGY	Have you got all day?
DONNA	Behave, Margy.
MARGY	You wouldn't be asking if I was fella though, would you? You wouldn't even mention it. And right now . . . I have got other things on my plate. The association, that's a big decision to make. And whichever way it goes . . . the way I see it. If it happens. It happens. It's meant to be. Alright.

(*Slight pause.*)

MARGY	Jamie-Lee. We're in the staggered lines and getting into this turn-about . . .
JAMIE-LEE	You're messing.
MARGY	It won't take long. If you could just stand in for us.
DONNA	Stand in?
MARGY	Only here. You can bring the baby, I don't mind.

(MARGY *takes up her place, as before.*)

MARGY	Only what it is. From the staggered lines, the three-lines-of-four if we go into a sort of two spread out two-groups-of-four. Same arm-movements as last year. Side diamonds different. Two at either.
DONNA	Same arm-movements?

(MARGY *manoeuvres* DONNA *and the pram into position.*)

MARGY	Yeah. I'll count it alright. Marking it through . . .

(Margy *takes up her place. She prepares to
dance as before.* Sharon *enters. She eats a hot
dog, smothered in ketchup.*)

Sharon   Could I find a painkiller from no one? Not a
                single, decent, living person.

Margy   Number six, please.

Sharon   Look at it. I had to get this in the end.

Margy   Sharon. And watch your dress.

Sharon   Are you still here?

                (Sharon *walks on, straight through their
                routine positions.*)

Margy   I'm talking to you.

Sharon   I just never realised how hungry I was. Dizzy.

Margy   Sharon . . .

Sharon   (*she sits, drinks*) And dehydrated . . .

Margy   I won't ask you again.

Sharon   (*sighs*) Margy. Haven't you got a complaint to
                be official about or something?

Donna   Margy, are we doing this or what?

                (*Still eating,* Sharon *moves into her position.*)

Margy   Right. From the staggered lines, girls. Into the
                diamonds.

                (Margy *begins to practise step. The others
                follow. The move and arm-movements are
                exactly the same as previous. At that moment,
                part of the arm movement,* Sharon *pushes her
                arm forward.* Sharon's *hot dog collides with*
                Jamie-Lee's *dress. Instantly, ketchup is
                smeared.*)

SHARON	Fuck.
MARGY	Sharon!
JAMIE-LEE	Sharon . . .
MARGY	Oh frig.
SHARON	Oh frig.
JAMIE-LEE	And you know who my mum'll blame, don't you?
MARGY	Don't I.
JAMIE-LEE	Margy.
MARGY	Donna . . . hurry up.
JAMIE-LEE	The state of it.
MARGY	Turn around.
SHARON	It'll come out. Won't it.

(*Using* DONNA'S *baby-wipes,* MARGY *rubs at the dress.*)

MARGY	Some Championship this is turning out to be. We haven't even had a troupe bloody practise.
SHARON	If it makes any difference, neither's Speke Jags. Still. On their arses, getting the ale in. And not a paracetamol between them. You think I'm bad. Marg, you want see it. There's is in two litre Diet Cokes. Makes you wonder where they get the money like, doesn't it. Doesn't it, Marg.

(MARGY *doesn't reply.*)

DONNA	If they've got the money for ale, Sha . . . Won't they want the cigarettes to go with it?
SHARON	Won't they. Donna . . .
JAMIE-LEE	Is it coming out?

DONNA   (*handing out wipes*) More?

MARGY   Jamie.

SHARON   One more scrub, Jame. It'll be alright.

               (JAMIE-LEE *reacts.*)

SHARON   I'm going.

               (SHARON *grabs up her holdall, gathers more
               stock.*)

JAMIE-LEE   That's right, yeah. Stick to what you're good
               at.

MARGY   Alright.

JAMIE-LEE   Sell your ciggies, sell your knock-off.

SHARON   Go on.

JAMIE-LEE   Chav trackies. Have you got any?

MARGY   Now, eh.

JAMIE-LEE   No. 'Cos of her. I haven't even got a dress.

SHARON   Yeah, and you're not used to that are you,
               babe. Trainer's daughter, always favouritised.

JAMIE-LEE   No I'm not.

SHARON   That's what your mates think, is it? Why aren't
               you hanging round with them, Jamie-Lee?

               (SHARON *exits.*)

JAMIE-LEE   I used to like coming here. What happened, eh?

MARGY   God knows.

               (*Pause.*)

DONNA   She could always like, have my dress you
               know.

MARGY	Donna. The last time I saw your dress . . .
DONNA	Lily told me. She still brings it and everything. Every week. It's on the bus.
MARGY	Your dress?
DONNA	I never knew I meant that much to her. For her to keep my own uniform.
MARGY	Jamie-Lee. Shape.
DONNA	The spare dressbag. It's there if you need it.
	(MARGY *fetches* JAMIE-LEE'S *tracksuit. She proceeds to undress* JAMIE-LEE, *removing her dress and stepping her into the tracksuit. It is a well-practised move.*)
MARGY	In this and over the bus . . . Hurry up.
JAMIE-LEE	There's a field of people.
MARGY	No one can see.
JAMIE-LEE	Mind.
MARGY	We haven't got time to mind. Jamie.
JAMIE-LEE	What shall I do with this?
MARGY	Toilets. I'll rinse it through. Any permanent damage today, I couldn't cope. (*She moves away.*) And tell the rest of them to get moving while you're there.
JAMIE-LEE	Me? After the show I got made of before. Margy . . .
	(MARGY *deposits the large ckeck bag before* JAMIE-LEE.)
MARGY	Dressed and over here. Go on. Two more then us. We haven't got all day.
JAMIE-LEE	Do I have to?

MARGY   Yes.

MARGY   Eh. And tell Siobhan . . . her head. I'm not
             putting up with it any more.

             (JAMIE-LEE *exits.*)

DONNA   Siobhan. Has she really got nits?

MARGY   Wake up, Donna. Siobhan's always had nits.

             (MARGY *checks over the soiled dress. Over the
             tannoy, music from the arena plays: Tragedy
             by Steps, a remix version/ABBA medley.*)

MARGY   Right then. We must be a due a bit of luck
             somewhere today, mustn't we? See you, Don.

DONNA   See you.

             (MARGY *exits with the dress.* DONNA *sits alone.
             The music plays. At the pram,* DONNA *checks at
             the baby. She stands. She goes to the arena,
             she watches. After a moment,* DONNA *looks
             about. She just can't help herself.* DONNA *goes
             up on her toes and begins to march. She
             performs an arm-movement and breaks into
             dancing step. She dances. Suddenly aware of
             what she is doing,* DONNA *halts her dance.*
             DONNA *exits with the pram.*)

                         Scene Two

*The encampment. The same day. A little later. From the
tannoy, troupe music continues to play.*

MARGY *enters. Dressed as before, she carries* JAMIE-LEE'S *dress
with her. The dress is now wet through. Seeing no one around,*
MARGY *pauses. She looks about. She goes to the shaker sack.
Carefully, she checks underneath for any signs of life. From
her bag,* MARGY *takes out her mobile. She checks at it for
messages, puts it back. She brings out her headdress. After a
moment,* MARGY *wrings out* JAMIE-LEE'S *dress once more. She*

examines. The dress still bears an obvious stain. MARGY *goes to the arena. She watches. After a moment* LILY *enters.*

LILY   Well. The things you find out in a beer tent. What have I always told you?

                (*Away from* MARGY'S *sight,* LILY *puts her purse away.*)

LILY   Funny, isn't it? When I come back here before. And there was you with the blind cheek. Changing a move. I knew. The first thought in my head . . . you know what have I done to deserve this? Eh. I couldn't understand it at the time, like. But now? 'Cos if I hadn't took myself off for that little pick-me-up, next season, my troupe. Bloody struggling. Without their leader . . . living in your shadow, Margy. That's what we might have been doing. Well not any more. And d'you know why? Belief. This is one of them life changing days, this.

MARGY   Is it, yeah?

LILY   Yeah. It is. I bloody believed you, Margy. This grant. These forms.

MARGY   What about them?

LILY   The truth, Margy. After a few it all comes out.

                (*From* MARGY'S bag, LILY *retrieves the forms.*)

LILY   It's not just Speke Jags on the case this time you know.

MARGY   You what?

LILY   Milano. Sovereign. The whole lot . . . They're only applying for a community grant.

MARGY   Off who?

LILY   The frigging community.

MARGY   They're applying. Is that what they said?
          Bloody wild fire. How did this happen?

LILY   Don't ask me.

          (*She fingers at the forms.*)

MARGY   Give us them.

LILY   To you? No chance. You've had us bloody
          good style, you.

MARGY   Me?

          (LILY *gestures the forms.*)

LILY   I thought you was the only person capable.
          Only you're not are you. Clever Margy.
          Applying for funding.

MARGY   It was me who found out.

LILY   From now on, I am standing on my own two
          feet. If Milano can do it, the lot of them with
          bad bleeding teeth.

MARGY   They're my forms.

LILY   My troupe. I'm doing it my way. (*A pause.*)
          Least that woman from Milano knew what she
          was on about. Even if you're not illegible,
          you're illegible. Apply for everything.

MARGY   I already have. Everything we're eligible for
          anyway.

          (LILY *sits. She takes out a pen and studies the
          forms.*)

MARGY   Lily. What are you doing?

LILY   Making sure. Tick all the right boxes, a few
          more for good measure.

MARGY   You can't lie, Lily.

LILY	Can't I? This is cash we're talking here.
MARGY	And that's a legal document. Signed by me.
LILY	So? If they're all gonna do it . . . these bloody boxes.
MARGY	They're gonna do what?
LILY	Ethnic, race, culture. Represent the lot, she said.
MARGY	We don't.
LILY	We do.
MARGY	Like who? All of us. This isn't just pale Lily, this is Irish white. Sunbeds don't count.
LILY	Jodie's step-dad. Her half-brother, he's mixed-race.
MARGY	Her half-brother's got ginger hair.
LILY	The other one. You know. So say like if Jodie had a sister instead. If she wanted to join, she'd join, wouldn't she?
MARGY	Right.
LILY	Right. Where are these boxes, have you seen these bleeding boxes . . .

(MARGY *removes the forms from her*.)

MARGY	I think you'll find I've got it all covered actually, Lil. 'Our Lady All Angels' operates an 'open door policy'.
LILY	An open what?
MARGY	Pay a pound a week subs, you're in. Regardless of you know, anything.
LILY	You can't put that. (LILY *snatches the forms away*.) This is a troupe. You've got to draw the

line somewhere you know. Open frigging door
. . . What are you saying, if some poor mixed-
up lad wanted to join we'd have to let him?

MARGY   If he wanted.

LILY   If he wanted, he could go to some village with
a hanky and a big stick. And as for you know,
the others. If we ended up with any of them.

MARGY   What others?

LILY   Well you know. The poor like, handicapped
and that. Where would we be then, eh?

MARGY   Very satisfied probably. It can't all be about
competition now you know.

LILY   Look who's bleeding talking.

MARGY   Not if you want funding it can't.

(*Slight pause.*)

LILY   To think I've bloody fell for this. You and your
big, correct bleeding ways. I'll tell you
something, if you want a job bloody doing,
Lily . . .

(LILY *puts a line through the form.*)

MARGY   That's our constitution.

LILY   And from what you've put, it's worth nothing.
Not to us anyway. You know, there's some
people what's actually good at this, Margy.
Forms. Filling them in. That's what they do.
That's another thing I found out and all.
Rumour has it, next season. That's what Big
Joan's got lined up. A funding specialist. And
all the troupes, we'll all be able to go to her.
'Cos whoever she is, the woman's supposed to
be brilliant. About funding for morris as a
sport, or as a culture, she knows the lot.

(*On the form,* LILY *writes.*)

LILY   Morris. Dancing. Keeps. Kids . . . off the.
            Street. I bet you she'd tell you.

MARGY   I best fetch the girls. Next on, there's a lot to
            do.

            (MARGY *goes to the dress rail. At the dress
            rail,* MARGY *hangs up* JAMIE-LEE'S *dress,
            smooths it out.*)

LILY   That dress. Margy . . . what is that on that
            dress?

MARGY   Your Jamie-Lee's? You know what it's like
            round here. One uniform ruined, Sharon does a
            runner.

LILY   What have you been up to, eh? I come back
            here and not even Donna . . . What's up, she
            had a baby before you could even manage it?

MARGY   I've had enough.

LILY   Jealous. Her first day back, your last.

MARGY   Will you listen to yourself.

LILY   No, you wouldn't want Donna getting all the
            attention now, would you? Eh? Poor bloody
            Donna . . .

            (*At that moment,* DONNA *enters with the pram.
            She pauses.*)

MARGY   What was it, Donna's special dress what you
            bring every week? Isn't that what you told her?

LILY   Who told her?

MARGY   Buttering her up. Keep that up Lily, you'll soon
            have her back. Right where you want her.
            Washing the frocks and scrubbing the pumps.
            A nice girl. She won't say no.

(LILY *doesn't reply.*)

DONNA   I go to get the baby a medal. Her first ever
              attendance. Then this.

MARGY   She's trying to get you back. Your special
              dress. She'd say anything . . . Next thing, she'll
              be promising you the baby can be mascot next.
              Any kid, she always does.

              (*Slight pause.*)

DONNA   Lily . . .

MARGY   For God's sake.

LILY   Next year. A new leader.

MARGY   I'd like to see it.

LILY   Better than you.

MARGY   Out of our lot? You better start head-hunting.

LILY   You better start packing your bags.

              (*Slight pause.*)

MARGY   Leaving this morris. I should have done it
              years ago. Who'll run round after you now, eh?
              Like me, all these years and stupid enough . . .
              a bloody fool.

              (JAMIE-LEE *enters. Over her shoulder, she
              carries a dress bag.*)

JAMIE-LEE   Margy. I got the dress for you.

MARGY   Jamie.

JAMIE-LEE   Not that it was easy like. Standing there on my
              own bus. Getting laughed at.

LILY   What dress?

JAMIE-LEE   Everything I told them. I tried to explain.

DONNA	What happened?
MARGY	They are getting ready, aren't they?
JAMIE-LEE	They are, yeah.

(JAMIE-LEE *hands the dress bag to* MARGY.)

JAMIE-LEE	I thought you might be interested.
MARGY	Interested in what?
LILY	Jamie-Lee. I mean it now.
JAMIE-LEE	Have a look, go on.
LILY	Margy . . .
JAMIE-LEE	No. See for herself. That's what I've just done. In front of my so-called mates. Donna's dress, I go. It's in here. Only look what I pull out . . .

(*From the dress bag,* MARGY *takes out a dress. It is a leader's dress, an exact replica of the one she wears.*)

LILY	Jamie-Lee . . .
JAMIE-LEE	That's what it says on the label.

(MARGY *checks inside the dress.*)

MARGY	Jamie-Lee. Leader.
JAMIE-LEE	Don't look at me.
MARGY	For her? Her leader?
LILY	She's my daughter. It's only natural.
MARGY	I'm leader.
LILY	If you had a kid Margy, you'd do the same. It's the truth. If it wasn't for having our Jamie-Lee.
MARGY	I didn't make you give up.

LILY	No, but if you hadn't been there . . . had a baby. And that was me over with.
MARGY	My fault? How long have you been planning this? Her . . . instead of me.
JAMIE-LEE	Yeah. That's what they all said.

(JAMIE-LEE *takes up the dress.*)

JAMIE-LEE	The first I knew about it, I didn't know what to say. I'm standing there and there's them. Eeeh Jamie-Lee . . . your Ma. You as leader . . . Who d'you think you are? . . . You lead, girl, I'm packing in . . . What could I say? Just stand there and take it.

(LILY *interjects, attempts to snatch the dress.*)

LILY	What are you playing at? My spare dress bag.
JAMIE-LEE	It wasn't me put it there.
LILY	You shouldn't be snooping.
JAMIE-LEE	I was fetching a dress.
LILY	Messing things up. I know you.
JAMIE-LEE	No you don't. This. It isn't mine.

(JAMIE-LEE *thrusts the dress to* LILY. *She moves away, gathering her belongings.*)

LILY	Lads. That's what this is. I should have known you'd be up to something.
JAMIE-LEE	You weren't like? Making a dress. Behind my back.
LILY	It was meant to be a surprise.
JAMIE-LEE	It was. Sharon was right. Trainer's daughter always favouritised. All I am is laughed at. And there's you without a thought, making plans, for everyone. For me. For my life . . . you know.

I'm supposed to want to be leader, am I? How do you know?

LILY   My troupe. One day yours. It's your every right.

JAMIE-LEE   Margy. This is nothing to do with me.

LILY   No. It's to do with her. How old and still dancing . . . Favouritised? You've been waiting long enough.

JAMIE-LEE   It's you who's been waiting, Mum.

(JAMIE-LEE *picks up her belongings. She moves away.*)

LILY   Jamie-Lee . . . Jamie. Now eh. Eh?

(*At the banner,* JAMIE-LEE *disappears behind it. A pause.*)

MARGY   Me gone. That's all you wanted.

LILY   None of us can morris dance forever, Margy.

MARGY   I've played right into your hands.

(MARGY *walks away. She offers out her headdress to* DONNA, *for her to put it on her.*)

MARGY   Do us a favour would you, Don.

(*Pause.*)

LILY   Come on, Marg. All she had to do was tell me, you know. If our Jamie-Lee never wanted to be leader, that's all she had to do . . . Jame. D'you hear me? Do you hear that, babe? 'Cos what's one dress? If you'd have said. I wouldn't even have made it. I wouldn't have bothered. Marg . . . 'Cos you know what I'm like for her. Anything. Aren't I Jamie? You know . . . and when she was little. Senior Leader . . . Sweet Jesus. You set your heart on that. Didn't you? Me and you. One day, you used to say. And

that's what I thought . . . one day. There was
nothing in it, I just always thought . . . you
know. I mean, for frig's sake. Jamie-Lee, we
could at least like, talk about it. Me and you.
Like adults. We could sit down and that.
Honest to God, 'cos the thought of you
missing out . . .

(*From the banner,* JAMIE-LEE *emerges.*)

JAMIE-LEE   Don't you ever listen?

LILY   Love. There's nothing worse than regrets.

             (JAMIE-LEE *steps out. She is wearing her
             'civvies' – a trendy, intelligent teenager.*)

LILY   Now hang on a minute.

JAMIE-LEE   No. Mum, no matter what you say. I come over
             here to tell you.

             (JAMIE-LEE *hands over her troupe tracksuit.*)

JAMIE-LEE   It isn't me any more.

LILY   Jamie. No.

JAMIE-LEE   Mum.

LILY   Just this one thing. Senior leader.

JAMIE-LEE   Will you . . .

LILY   For me then.

JAMIE-LEE   Will you tell her.

LILY   You can't do this, Jamie.

JAMIE-LEE   It doesn't work like that.

MARGY   Leave it, Lil.

LILY   Work like what?

JAMIE-LEE	You was never Leader of the Year. It doesn't mean me.
LILY	I know that.
JAMIE-LEE	You don't though. You never have.
	(*Pause.*)
LILY	Jamie. This is nothing to do with winning, this. You can win if you like. But if you don't . . .
	(JAMIE-LEE *reacts.*)
LILY	This is us, it's what we do.
JAMIE-LEE	It's what you do. I'm your girl. I'm not you. I don't want to make a life out of your morris. It doesn't mean I don't love you like . . . you know.
LILY	I know. Jamie . . .
JAMIE-LEE	I've got to go, mum.
	(JAMIE-LEE *gathers her belongings.*)
LILY	Now. Jamie . . . where are you going?
JAMIE-LEE	He's waiting in the car.
LILY	Who's waiting?
	(JAMIE-LEE *goes to* LILY. *She kisses her on the cheek.*)
JAMIE-LEE	I'll see you at home.
LILY	Jamie . . .
	(JAMIE-LEE *exits.*)
LILY	Jame . . . Jamie.
	(*Pause.*)

MARGY   Come on, Lil. They all go through this one.
             Even me. Till I found my fella.

DONNA   Early days. You know what they're like.

LILY   Not her. No. She won't come back. She won't.
             We've all seen enough girls to know.

             (*A pause.* LILY *moves away. She sets down*
             JAMIE-LEE'S *tracksuit.*)

LILY   Her gone. You gone. What am I gonna do now,
             eh?

             (*Over the tannoy, troupe music starts to play.*
             No Dream Impossible, by Lindsay D. After a
             moment, an announcement is heard.)

BIG JOAN   Ladies and Gentlemen, next on the arena.
             Toxteth Debutantes. Our Lady All Angels'
             please get ready, please, Our Ladies.

MARGY/LILY/ (*they chant, automatic*) Our Ladies, winning is
DONNA   our ease.

LILY   Not with one dancer bloody short it's not.

             (*Between* MARGY *and* LILY, *an exchange of*
             looks. DONNA *reaches the water bottle of*
             alcohol. For courage, she takes a large swig.)

                         Scene Three

Later. The same day.

The encampment stands empty. At the dress rail, JAMIE-LEE'S
leader's dress now hangs. Over the tannoy, troupe music
plays. After a moment, an announcement is heard, applause.

BIG JOAN   A big round of applause please, Our Lady All
             Angels'. Thank you Our Lady All Angels'.

             (*Off, a chant is heard, singing. A troupe at*
             first, voices trail away.)

THE TROUPE   (*off, they sing*)

                  We are Our Lady's girls . . . Everybody knows!
                  We know our manners, we earn our tanners,
                  We are respected wherever we may go.
                  And when we travel on a corpie bus,
                  Doors and windows open wide.
                  We know how to lift our feet,
                  Morris dancing is our treat.

                  We are Our Lady's girls . . .
                  Hello, hello, hello, hello,
                  We are Our Lady's girls . . .
                  Hello, hello, hello, hello,
                  We are Our Lady's girls.

                  (SHARON *and* DONNA *enter. Both exhausted and
                  fully dressed from dancing,* SHARON'S *dress is
                  fully open at the back. Still singing, their
                  chant is workaday.*)

DONNA/SHARON . . . And if you are another troupe surrender or
                  you die. 'Cos we are the greatest . . . Our
                  Lady's!

                  (SHARON *throws down her shakers, tired out.*)

SHARON   I thought I was gonna die myself.

DONNA   You did. Your face.

SHARON   Er . . . your's was bad enough. I looked at you
                  checking my spacing.

DONNA   No way.

SHARON   No messing girl. When we go up-up in them
                  diagonal lines.

DONNA   I never even looked at you.

SHARON   Good job you never. Donna. Panic.

                  (SHARON *pulls a face. They laugh.*)

SHARON   Honest to God . . . I nearly pissed myself.

DONNA   Aaah, no. It wasn't that bad.

                (DONNA *deposits their shakers at the sack.*
                SHARON *kicks off her pumps.*)

SHARON   Donna. It was. Your bleeding gob.

DONNA   Did I look how you felt?

                (DONNA *turns,* SHARON *undoes her zip.*)

SHARON   Tell me about it. We'd only just gone into
                dancing and I was like that . . . Knobhead.
                Forgot my inhaler.

DONNA   I thought I heard you gasping.

SHARON   Out of condition. I was fighting for my life.

                (SHARON *sits to the ground, exhausted. She
                pulls off her socks, takes her arms out her
                dress to cool off.*)

SHARON   Two weeks, no dance. Jesus . . .

                (SHARON *reaches her alcohol, she drinks.*)

DONNA   I wondered what was up with you. Then when
                we come off I knew you was gonna spew.

SHARON   I knew I was gonna spew.

DONNA   Either that or I thought I'd done crap.

                (SHARON *takes a drink. She pours another
                drink into a plastic cup.*)

SHARON   Better . . . Don?

                (DONNA *hesitates.*)

SHARON   One little bit's not gonna do any harm.

DONNA   Oh. Go on then.

SHARON   The morris.

DONNA   I know yeah.

                (DONNA *sips.* SHARON *lies back, exhausted. She*
                reaches for her food.)

DONNA   It was an alright dance, though. Wasn't it? I
                was alright?

                (SHARON *doesn't reply. She continues to eat.*
                After a moment, LILY *enters pushing the pram.*
                A pile of shakers are balanced on top, more in
                the tray beneath.)

LILY   Our Ladys'!

DONNA   How is she Lil? Still okay for you?

LILY   Well away.

                (LILY *parks up the pram. Removing some*
                shakers, she deposits them close to the sack.)

DONNA   What about the dance? Was that okay and all?

LILY   Donna, I told you.

DONNA   I know but. The championships. Who goes on
                and does practise step. I felt ashamed.

LILY   Special circumstances. You done bleeding
                great.

DONNA   And I won't get marked down for not dancing
                properly, will I?

LILY   Donna. I cleared it. Alright. I even went to Big
                Joan and I told her. That girl's just dropped.
                She's got stitches.

DONNA   I never had stitches.

LILY   You might as well for all she knows. Just for
                you, alright. And that's some achievement that.
                Me, her, d'you know what I mean?

DONNA   Ta, Lil.

LILY   And Margy. And if Margy told her, Big Joan
             and her new best friend to be.

DONNA   Ta very much.

LILY   Like any girl. You only done practise step 'cos
             you had to. Next time, you can dance.

DONNA   Next time?

             (*Close to the pram,* LILY *lights up a cigarette.*)

LILY   If you want to help us out again like. No
             pressure or nothing. But I mean, the way you
             saved us today Don. Stepping in, last minute
             . . . I'll be keeping your dress forever now,
             won't I?

DONNA   Yeah. Well if I done alright . . . yeah.

             (*Still smoking,* LILY *begins to push at the
             pram.* DONNA *hesitates.*)

DONNA   'Cos I did think like. On there . . . I did think. I
             think I know what I'm doing. For the first time,
             you know, in ages. Like everything was just
             right. On there, it was as if something just come
             over me or something.

LILY   That's how she was and all. Soon as she heard
             our music.

DONNA   Go 'way.

LILY   She was off.

SHARON   You sure it wasn't boredom?

LILY   She loved it alright. Just like her mother.

             (DONNA *moves away. She sits, her back turned
             to the pram.*)

DONNA   I might only have been doing practise step but
                 . . . that dance. I knew she was with Lily and
                 she was alright . . . even in that dead hard
                 move. You know the one where I move. A bit.
                 Then move again.

LILY   The continuous.

DONNA   That. Where I end up in line with you, Sha.
                 Before we went on, I was petrified.

SHARON   Which move's this?

DONNA   The one where I move. You know.

LILY   The continuous.

                 (DONNA *stands, casually demonstrating an
                 arm-movement, moving then turning.*)

DONNA   To here. I end up in line with you.

SHARON   Jamie-Lee's place?

DONNA   Yeah.

SHARON   You don't end up in line with me.

DONNA   I did.

                 (*Over the tannoy an announcement is heard.*)

BIG JOAN   Ladies and Gentlemen, a warm, very warm
                 Championship welcome. Our next troupe of the
                 day . . . Speke Jaguar.

                 (*They applaud. Troupe music plays.*)

LILY   Go on then. If I bleeding have to.

                 (LILY *applauds.* SHARON *stands.*)

SHARON   Pissheads. I hope they make a show.

                 (LILY *paces, watching the troupes.*)

DONNA	Sharon . . .
LILY	Gets on my tit.
DONNA	What you said.
SHARON	What d'you reckon, Lil?
LILY	What do I reckon?
DONNA	Sharon. You could at least have given me the nod.
SHARON	The what?
DONNA	That continuous. If I was lined up with you . . .
SHARON	I never really noticed.
DONNA	I thought I'd done good.
SHARON	Didn't we all.

(DONNA *moves away, she sits*.)

SHARON	Donna . . . what do you want? Me to move you, is that it? Me to get marked down for big illegal head signals . . . (SHARON *nods, side-to-side, over-earnest*.) 'Donna. Donna . . .'. Sorry love, if you went wrong that's Margy's job to correct you. That's what a leader's for you know. That's up to Margy.
LILY	Margy's what?
SHARON	Ask her.
DONNA	Two minutes practise. No one even told me to move.
LILY	Move where?
SHARON	For frig's sake. (SHARON *drinks once more*.) It's alright. I have danced.
DONNA	I was in line with her.

SHARON   Yeah. Only she shouldn't have been.

                (DONNA *goes to the pram.*)

DONNA   I knew this. If we do crap, who's fault will it be.
                I'm going home.

                (SHARON *tuts.* DONNA *fastens her dress.*)

LILY   Donna . . . so you might have messed up.

SHARON   She did mess up.

LILY   Yeah. But it was Margy what did frig-all about
                it. You know. What's worse?

DONNA   Come on, babe.

LILY   Donna. There's no guessing what these judges
                make of us.

                (LILY *moves to arena, she observes.*)

DONNA   It would have been better without me though.
                Wouldn't it? You would have done better with
                your Jamie-Lee.

                (*Slight pause.*)

SHARON   What do they look like, Lily?

LILY   Slow but bleeding precise. This is a good
                dance they're having.

                (MARGY *enters. Dressed in full morris uniform,
                she carries her shakers and a music cassette.
                She deposits her shakers in the bag.*)

MARGY   Bloody'ell. Talk about getting trapped. Once
                that music's on, you know what Big Joan's like.
                I thought I'd never get out. She thought we
                done a really good job, anyway.

                (MARGY *goes on. Unzipping her dress she
                pauses, aware of their reaction.*)

MARGY	What . . . ?
DONNA	I messed up, Margy.
SHARON	And someone never corrected her. So whatever your big mate's been saying, not worth tuppence. You should have been doing your job.
MARGY	I was. I never corrected no one.
LILY	See what I mean.
MARGY	There was no one to correct. The new turn-about. Nothing.
LILY	You what?
MARGY	Well you saw it. Even in that dead hard move and that has been out all season. Not that it ever made the cards like but you know. These adjudicators sometimes . . . it takes a certain eye.
LILY	You can say that again.
MARGY	So yeah. Thanks to Donna.
SHARON	Her?
DONNA	Me? Are you sure?
MARGY	It was a good job you were here. 'Cos I'm not being funny, but . . . sometimes your Jamie-Lee's spacing . . . It did leave something to be desired, didn't it?
DONNA	Did it? Aaah.
LILY	Now hang on. Our Jamie-Lee?
MARGY	I told her many a time.
LILY	Not here to defend herself. You would drag her in.

MARGY	No. In that move. You know in that one . . .
	(MARGY *demonstrates a casual arm-movement, moving and turning as* DONNA *did earlier*.)
MARGY	She moves a bit then moves again. Ends up in line with Sharon.
SHARON	No.
DONNA	The continuous.
MARGY	You think about it. Same as your opposite partners. Jodie one side . . .
LILY	Dirty Siobhan the other.
MARGY	Only your Jamie-Lee . . .
LILY	She was never nowhere near.
MARGY	She never ended up in line with no one.
SHARON	Friggin'ell . . .
MARGY	It had been happening a while. We should have seen it coming . . . your daughter or not. She was losing interest.
LILY	Well d'you know what? When I get home . . . I knew there was something wrong with that move. I told you, didn't I? That continuous . . . My routines, you see. Too bleeding technical.
SHARON	Whose routines, Lil?
LILY	This troupe. You know.
	(MARGY *removes her pumps. She rubs at her feet*.)
MARGY	So yeah. That's what Big Joan reckons. We should be made up. A definite place she reckons.
DONNA	Oh my God.

MARGY	It's what we deserve. Maybe even a second, you never know.
LILY	Second? The way Speke are dancing? All my eye.
MARGY	That's what she said.
LILY	And you believed her? Them lines are perfect.
MARGY	Perfect or not, Lil. It doesn't matter what way Speke dance. But that's the sort of thing you find out when you're mates with Big Joan, isn't it?
LILY	What is?
MARGY	Inside info.
LILY	Oh aye? I bet that doesn't come for free does it. What did you tell her, Margy? Our Jamie-Lee, she hated every dance her own mother made her do.
MARGY	I wouldn't do that.
LILY	It was your last dance wasn't it. Between you and her. My own daughter and my morris mate. So much for bloody loyalty . . .

(*Slight pause.*)

MARGY	Actually Lily. It was loyalty why I did it. (*She pauses.*) The North-West and North Wales International Morris Dance Association voluntary funding consultant.
SHARON	What?
DONNA	Go 'way.
MARGY	Yeah. No judging, just sitting there. Giving out forms. Advice. Grant after grant, updating the webpage . . .

LILY   You. She wants you for that?

MARGY   Well, it's hardly me, is it. (*She pauses.*) Yeah
            . . . so that's what I told her anyway.

            (MARGY *moves away. She collects up the odd
            stray shaker.*)

MARGY   Any more shakers for the bag anyone . . .

SHARON   You mean. You turned her down?

DONNA   Margy. That was your future.

LILY   Future . . . don't talk soft. She's a girl from Our
            Lady's. This is where she belongs.

MARGY   That's what I said.

LILY   I hope you did, girl.

MARGY   I did. 'Cos let's face it. A senior leader needs
            to give her all, doesn't she.

LILY   Doesn't she? You do. Helping me.

MARGY   If you'll have me, like. After all what I said
            before.

LILY   After all what you've said all day. Bloody'ell.
            Margy . . .

            (LILY *approaches her. But instead of an
            embrace, she picks up a troupe bag, passes it
            to* MARGY.)

MARGY   I know Lil, but . . .

LILY   Spare headdresses. We might need them.

MARGY   Lily . . . there just might need to be changes.
            That's all.

LILY   Changes? You're back leading aren't you.
            What sort of changes? Eh? And what did she

say to that, eh? Big Joan. I wish I'd have seen her face.

MARGY   You know . . . down all her chins. To be honest, I think she had her mind on other things. (*She smiles.*) Gossip of the year. I still managed to get that out of her, like.

LILY   You never?

MARGY   Inside info.

LILY   Have you heard this?

MARGY   Wait till you do.

LILY   I need a ciggie.

SHARON   Go on.

MARGY   Are you ready for this?

LILY   Hang on.

MARGY   Oh my God . . . (*She laughs.*) Speke Jags. Their leader, their back girl and see her – their number nine. Caught. Having a spliff behind the back of the committee caravan.

SHARON   Behave?

         (LILY *whoops.*)

LILY   Speke Jags . . .

MARGY   Swore me to secrecy.

DONNA   A proper spliff?

MARGY   What d'you think of that then?

SHARON   A spliff. Are you sure?

MARGY   This dance is just for punishment. Disqualified. They don't even know it.

LILY   You are having me on?

MARGY   (*clicking her fingers*) Like that.

             (*They observe the arena.*)

LILY   Fancy throwing away your Championship.

DONNA   On drugs. I mean there's kids round here.

LILY   Speke on drugs.

MARGY   Joan's argument exactly.

LILY   A bloody spliff. In public.

MARGY   And the smell of it. Apparently . . .

LILY   Go 'way.

SHARON   Margy. It wasn't a spliff. (*She pauses.*) I had to
             off load them herbal smokes somewhere. The
             packet's all in Turkish, they never knew what
             they was buying. I told them they was like
             B&H.

MARGY   Like bloody something. Sharon.

SHARON   They're not drugs.

LILY   I hope they're not.

SHARON   They just fucking stink. Eh Margy, she's not
             calling the bizzies, is she? If asks them to
             name the dealer. My poor kids.

             (SHARON *hurries to her holdall. She covers the
             bag, disguising it as best she can.*)

LILY   Speke Jags? They wouldn't dare.

SHARON   Disqualified. They'd say anything. If anyone
             comes, this isn't here alright.

LILY   They've done worse.

MARGY   We have. Second place. What did I tell you.

DONNA   Second. And there's me with the baby.

MARGY   Behind Wigan Pierettes I reckon.

LILY   Second? Come on, Margy. Aim bloody high,
               will you.

MARGY   (*gathering herself, once more*) Alright so it's
               not the double. But after what we've been
               through . . .

LILY   Exactly. What we've been through for all them
               years. Let's see how they'll like it for a change.
               Seeing us win when we shouldn't.

               (*From the tray of* DONNA's *pram,* LILY *holds up
               a nappy bag.*)

LILY   Second? Chuck this by the tent. The mood Big
               Joan's in, Wigan Pierettes' won't even touch
               the bloody floor.

SHARON   (*she laughs*) Lily . . .

LILY   In for a penny, in for a championship win.

MARGY   You wouldn't.

DONNA   That's one of hers.

LILY   Wouldn't I?

DONNA   It's blatant cheating.

MARGY   Lily, you can't. The name of this troupe.

               (MARGY *grabs the nappy sack from her.*)

LILY   I think you better get yourself over the fair
               then, hadn't you.

MARGY   Over the what?

LILY   One ride I said. They were upset over our
               Jamie.

MARGY   They're on the fair?

LILY   It'll do them good.

MARGY   In troupe dresses?

LILY   Well? That's what your grant's for, isn't it?

MARGY   For crying out loud . . .

             (MARGY *takes out her mobile. She goes to
             make a call.*)

MARGY   You knew it was full-dressed Grand Parade.
             Five minutes, the whole troupe or a point
             docked for every girl what's missing . . .
             Sharon. They won't answer me.

             (SHARON *reaches her mobile. She texts.* MARGY
             begins to remove the banner.)

MARGY   If we're not careful, we won't stand a bloody
             chance.

SHARON   How d'you spell 'gonna'? Margy gonna kick
             your arse.

MARGY   Second. Kiss goodbye to that.

DONNA   Says who?

MARGY   Associations rules, Don.

DONNA   No way. All my trouble. I want at least a medal
             out of this.

             (DONNA *pushes the pram to* MARGY.)

DONNA   'Ere y'are, Marg. I'll find them.

MARGY   (*she calls*) Donna . . . Two minutes. Tell them I
             said.

             (DONNA *exits. Immediately,* LILY *pushes the
             pram away from* MARGY.)

LILY	Eh. And now you're the expert. You better keep our application well under your hat. No letting it slip to Big Joan this time.
MARGY	I never did.
LILY	Well someone must have.
	(*Slight pause.*)
SHARON	Gossip. I thought I might have got a sale out of it. I never thought bleeding judge as well.
MARGY	Sharon. You what?
SHARON	Big Joan. Troupe trackies she goes to me. Round this arena. Everyone'll buy them in bulk. My tit they will. She wasn't even gonna put her hand in her pocket for a packet of twenty.
LILY	I'm warning you.
SHARON	I'm warned.
	(MARGY *picks up the banner.*)
MARGY	Right then. Grand Parade. Are you ready?
	(*From the pram,* LILY *holds up the nappy bag once more.*)
LILY	Grand Parade. There's gonna be some aggro now.
MARGY	Lily. No.
	(*Checking about,* LILY *tosses the nappy bag.*)
LILY	Go on, Sha. Throw it and run.
MARGY	You are having me on.
LILY	Why? What else are we gonna win, sweariest bleeding troupe?

MARGY   You can't.

LILY   Win the double. It's what you wanted.

MARGY   Not like this.

SHARON   They'd do it to us, Marg.

MARGY   Sharon.

SHARON   If it works, girls. It bleeding works. Joan's tent.
             I'll see you over there.

             (SHARON *exits.*)

MARGY   What would you do. This troupe . . .

LILY   Frig off, Margy. You love us really.

             (MARGY *takes up a troupe bag. Automatically,*
             LILY *hands out her folded chair.*)

MARGY   Lily . . . and don't forget them shakers.

LILY   Give us some credit, will you. How long have I
             been doing this?

             (MARGY *exits.* LILY *picks up the shaker bag*
             and goes to follow. Over the tannoy, music
             starts to play: Simply The Best by Tina
             Turner.)

LILY   Margy. Marg. Save us a good spec, will you?

             (LILY *puts down the shaker bag. She lights a*
             cigarette. Seeing the pram, she returns to fetch
             it. LILY *exits with the pram, past the shaker*
             bag. Lights fade.)

             End of play.

Author's Notes

Visually, female Morris Dancing has very little in common with the more well-known Men's Morris – and indeed is often frowned upon by such traditionalists. This female form of 'carnival' morris dancing is a past-time peculiar to only the North-West of England and North Wales. Its origins date back to the turn of the 20th century with its popularity and notoriety spreading through the customary annual fairs and parades of many North-West villages and towns until eventually competitive Morris became a regular feature on many carnival fields. However, little is known about carnival Morris Dancing nationally.

Organised and run on a voluntary basis, it is a popular hobby amongst girls of all ages with dancing taking place through different age-group sections – from baby troupes to dinkies, tiny, junior and eventually senior sections. There are no upper or lower age limits.

Dancing takes place in troupes of approximately twelve girls (it is always of an even number). A dancing display consists of a 'march-on' or entrance, followed by a routine in a different step such as the kick-out or the cross-over. At this point the troupe perform a flowing series of different formations along with arm-work using shakers or pom-poms. A march-off, or exit, from the dancing arena then completes the dance. An entire routine can sometimes last twelve minutes. A troupe leader keeps check on the routine, dancing at its centre and giving signals to the troupe where necessary by way of her shakers (or tambourine in younger sections).

Today, Morris Dancing competitions are often internalised affairs, taking place in sports halls and the like during the early and late months of the March-November season, and on grassy outdoor spaces in between. These outdoor competitions are often found on showgrounds, incorporated into either a traditional carnival or more frequently into a more commercial 'fun-day' event, complete with radio station roadshows, fairgrounds, market stalls, etc.

Most information regarding Morris Dancing can now be found via the internet, with dancing associations and a majority of troupes now possessing their own websites. Sites worth a visit include: www.morrisdancing.net (a comprehensive guide to all things Morris, including many troupe and association links) and www.lancashirecarnivalassociation.com.

THE MORRIS
First published in 2005
by Josef Weinberger Ltd
12-14 Mortimer Street, London, W1T 3JJ

ISBN 0 85676 281 4

Printed by Biddles Ltd, King's Lynn, Norfolk